THOUGHT CATALOG BOOKS

The Search For Something More

The Search For Something More

A Guide For Those Trying To Heal Themselves

RANIA NAIM

THOUGHT CATALOG BOOKS

Brooklyn, NY

THOUGHT CATALOG BOOKS

Copyright © 2016 by The Thought & Expression Co.

All rights reserved. Published by Thought Catalog Books, a division of The Thought & Expression Co., Williamsburg, Brooklyn. Founded in 2010, Thought Catalog is a website and imprint dedicated to your ideas and stories. We publish fiction and non-fiction from emerging and established writers across all genres. For general information and submissions: manuscripts@thoughtcatalog.com.

First edition, 2016

ISBN 978-1532874154

10 9 8 7 6 5 4 3 2 1

Cover photography by © LookCatalog.com

Contents

Part III. When Friends Become Family & Family Becomes Friends

Part IV. The Journey To Becoming Who You Really Are

Part 1

Falling in Love

Your task is not to seek for love, but merely to seek and find all the barriers within yourself that you have built against it.

– Rumi

1

40 Deep Questions To Ask If You Really Want To Get To Know Someone

1. What's your philosophy in life?

2. What's the one thing you would like to change about yourself?

3. Are you religious or spiritual?

4. Do you consider yourself an introvert or an extrovert?

5. Which parent are you closer to and why?

6. What was the best phase in your life?

7. What was the worst phase in your life?

8. Is what you're doing now what you always wanted to do growing up?

9. What makes you feel accomplished?

10. What's your favorite book/movie of all time and why did it speak to you so much?

11. What is a relationship deal breaker for you?

12. Are you more into looks or brains?

13. Would you ever take back someone who cheated?

14. How do you feel about sharing your password with your partner?

15. When do you think a person is ready for marriage?

16. What kind of parent do you think you will be?

17. What would you do if your parents didn't like your partner?

18. Who is that one person you can talk to about just anything?

19. Do you usually stay friends with your exes?

20. Have you ever lost someone close to you?

21. If you are in a bad mood, do you prefer to be left alone or have someone to cheer you up?

22. What's an ideal weekend for you?

23. What do you think of best friends of the opposite sex?

24. Do you judge a book by its cover?

25. Are you confrontational?

26. When was the last time you broke someone's heart?

27. Would you relocate for love?

28. Did you ever write a journal?

29. What are you most thankful for?

30. Do you believe in second chances?

31. What's the one thing that people always misunderstand about you?

32. What is your idea of a perfect vacation?

33. What did your past relationship teach you?

34. What are your thoughts on online dating or *tinder*?

35. What's on your bucket list this year?

36. When have you felt your biggest adrenaline rush?

37. What is the craziest thing you've ever done and would you do it again?

38. If a genie granted you 3 wishes right now, what would you wish for?

39. What's your biggest regret in life?

40. What do you think about when you're by yourself?

2

What I Really Wish I Could Tell You

I look at you with a smile on my face and say *'it's good to see you'* – but what I truly wish I could say is why are you talking to me? I wish I could ask you if you know who you are talking to or are you fooled like everyone else? I wish I could ask you if you are strong enough to keep up with me or is it a matter of time till you run away?

I wish I could tell you I am not used to being loved, I am not used to being treated like a queen and put on a pedestal. I am not used to someone showing up on my doorstep with roses.

I am not used to getting picked up on time, going on fancy dinner dates and receiving loving messages after every date. I am not used to feeling special. I am not used to feeling like my opinions matter and my thoughts count. **I am not used to the way you look at me.**

I wish I could tell you that I am really strong but really soft at the same time and I still don't know what triggers each of them. I wish I knew how to describe myself to you so you don't have to struggle so much with trying to define me. I wish you could understand that I want to let you in but I am still trying to see if you are really willing to cross the line.

I wish I could tell you that the reason why I'm so attached to my friends is that they are the ones who truly accepted me when I almost gave up on myself. I can't explain why they love me but they do and I wish I could get the same love from you.

I wish I could tell you that my family put me through hell but I survived, and it took me a while to learn to love them again, this is why I may not know how a family functions and I'm terrified of having one. **I wish I could tell you that at one point having a family was all I ever wanted but somehow that changed along the way.**

I wish I could tell you that I hated being alone or lonely and I looked for love in all the wrong places, this is why I'm comfortable with my loneliness now, it's now more of an *old friend* than an enemy. I wish you understood how long it took me to reach this point and how hard it is for me to give it up for someone temporary.

I wish I could tell you I am guarded because the one before you broke down all my walls and left me to deal with the *ruins* and I had to slowly rebuild it brick by brick. It is so hard for me to break them down again even though I really want to.

I wish I could tell you about how he wasted my time and made me feel worthless, about the days he wasn't there and the nights he disappeared, I wish I could tell you how weak I was with him. After that, *I vowed never to feel like that again.*

I wish I could tell you that if you don't plan to love me or take me seriously then please leave now because I am not going to give you my heart if you only want to play with it.

But I also wish I could tell you that if you plan to love me, I plan to love you harder and I will find the place in my heart where I once believed in eternal love and family, the place that is pure and free from all the agony and the pain.

If you plan to love me, I promise to find the right words to describe my feelings and help you unravel the puzzle of my life. If you plan to love me, I will slowly start breaking my own walls brick by brick and leave the door open for you.

If you plan to love me, I will slowly walk away from the comfort of my own loneliness and start embracing companionship again. **If you plan to love me, I promise you with all my heart, I will forget about anyone who came before you and you will be the *only* one.**

I wish I could tell you all that but I sip my coffee instead and ask you *'How was your day?'*

3

I Want To Listen To You Every Day Of The Week

I want to listen to you on Monday. I want to listen to you talk about your hectic day at work, about your annoying coworkers, about your lunch hour and about the projects you are working on. I want to listen to you talk about your achievements, your accomplishments, your ambitions, your goals and your future.

I want to listen to you on Tuesday. I want to listen to the stories about your family, the memories of your childhood and the struggles you had growing up. I want to listen to you talk about your friends, the ones you still talk to, the ones you no longer stay in touch with, the ones who hurt you and the ones who stood by your side. I want to listen to *who you are* as a friend.

I want to listen to you on Wednesday. I want to listen to the music you like and the words that move you. I want to listen to you sing even if you can't follow the note. I want to listen to the songs you've written when you were alone, when you tried to be artistic, when you didn't even know you were trying. I want to listen to your melody; to your *words*.

I want to listen to you on Thursday. I want to listen to your thoughts. Your complex, intriguing, deep and intrusive thoughts. I want to listen to your thoughts about life and how your mind connects the dots. I want to listen to your thoughts about people and if you think they're beautiful. But more than anything, I want to listen to your thoughts about *yourself* and if you truly like who you are when no one is around.

I want to listen to you on Friday. I want to listen to your heartbreak, your bad romance, your painful love stories and the one that got away. I want to listen to how you used to love and how you love now, how you used to care and how you care now and if the heartbreak has changed you at all. I want to listen to you talk about love and what truly touches your *fragile* heart.

I want to listen to you on Saturday. I want to listen to you open up after a few drinks, after the stress of the week is over, after the tough stories have been told. I want to listen to your laugh and the times you went crazy. I want to listen to your jokes and all the funny things that happened to you. I want to listen to you unfiltered, unplugged and unreserved. I want to listen to your *vulnerability* and the softness in your voice when you speak from the heart.

I want to listen to you on Sunday. I want to listen to you on Sunday morning when you are happy and relaxed, still trying to remember what happened the night before. I want to listen to you on Sunday evening when you are fretting about the busy week ahead and the obligations you have. I want to listen to your moody and agitated voice and try to calm you down with mine. But mainly, I want to listen to you on Sunday *night*, when you are not saying anything at all, when you are quiet, when you are tired, when you are pre-occupied, when you are restless and when you don't feel like saying a word. *I want to listen to you when you say nothing at all.*

And when the sun comes out, I'll be happy to listen to you all over again.

4

10 Ways To Open Up To Love Again After You've Been Hurt

It can be very hard to open up to love again after you've been hurt. I understand because I've been there. When we get disappointed, the natural tendency is to want to give up on love. But if we don't allow ourselves to open up to love again, we can miss out on the good things in life and we can miss out on the chance of finding the love we truly strive for. Here are ten ways to help you open up to love again.

1. Think of heartbreak as something of the past.

You can't take the heartbreak with you wherever you go, it can be hard to forget it but it doesn't have to be the first thought that comes to your mind whenever you meet someone who has potential. The person who broke your heart in the past has nothing to offer you in the present, so why let them shape your future?

2. Trust the universe.

What if life has better plans for you? Plans that don't involve tears and heartaches. This is why the only way we can trust the universe is to let go of what we can't change, or stop trying to change someone who is not willing to.

3. Take the lessons.

The truth is sometimes you have to get knocked down to learn how to stand back up. To open up to love again, you have to look at the lessons your heartbreak taught you about yourself; maybe it taught you to trust your intuition or to love yourself more, or maybe it taught you how to walk away or when to draw the line. Learning from your past mistakes is the only way you can lead yourself to find love you deserve rather than crumbs of love.

4. Don't take your bitterness or your resentment.

It can be easy to think everyone's out to get you when you've been hurt before, but instead of being stuck on the pain and everything that went wrong, allow yourself the power of forgiveness and remind yourself that whoever hurt you was not an evil person, they just weren't the best person for *you*.

5. Understand that closing your heart off is not going to make you any happier.

It's normal–even healthy to have some walls up, but to close yourself off completely and have a negative outlook on love is only going to set you up for regret and misery. *The grass is not always greener on the safe side.*

6. Be honest with yourself.

Be honest with yourself about what went wrong, sometimes it's you and sometimes it's them. Sometimes it's timing and sometimes it's your own fears and insecurities. If you can be honest with yourself about what exactly went wrong and pin down how you contributed to it, you are more likely to avoid these mistakes in the future.

7. Accept that love will always be risky.

Opening up to someone or falling in love with someone will always be risky and the outcome will never be guaranteed, but as with everything in life, some things are totally worth the risk, sometimes taking the risk is the only way you can actually feel *alive*.

8. Take your time.

Take your time to heal. Take your time to get to know someone new. Take your time to listen to your heart and pay close attention to your feelings. Take your time to open up to love again so you can make sure you are ready for the right kind of love when it knocks on your door.

9. Let go of comparisons.

Comparing yourself to others, or comparing others to your ex will only impede you from enjoying the moment. Don't judge a book by its cover and don't be so hard on yourself. We are each on our own journeys and we should trust that our story will eventually have a happy ending.

10. Remember that you are lovable.

Think of all the people who love you and the people who think highly of you. Think of the good things you do for people and the ways you support your friends and family. Think of how you keep trying to be a better person; let these be reminders that you are a person worthy of love and that you deserve *phenomenal* love.

5

30 Ways You Can Tell The Difference Between Love And Infatuation

I always thought infatuation is part of love, I thought they complement each other until I experienced both and discovered that they can't coexist. There are too many people who are convinced that they're in love with someone just because they're amazing and they can't stop thinking about them, but the truth is most of the time the intensity that comes with really liking someone is not love-it's infatuation. Here are some ways to tell the difference.

1. Infatuation happens instantly. Love is a slow process.

2. Infatuation craves physical affection. Love craves a deeper connection.

3. Infatuation makes you act irrationally or 'crazy.' Love calms you down.

4. Infatuation is intense but short-lived. Love is comfortable but lasts longer.

5. Infatuation is reckless with our emotions. Love is more considerate.

6. Infatuation has ulterior motives. Love has genuine intentions.

7. Infatuation brings out obsession and jealousy. Love brings out understanding and trust.

8. Infatuation is shallow. Love is deep.

9. Infatuation is selfish and draining. Love is kind and energizing.

10. Infatuation makes a big deal out of small things. Love lets them go.

11. Infatuation is being in love with the idea of someone. Love is being in love with who the person really is.

12. Infatuation is possessive. Love is generous.

13. Infatuation holds grudges. Love forgives.

14. Infatuation keeps you guessing. Love answers your questions.

15. Infatuation thrives on playing games. Love thrives on meaningful connections.

16. Infatuation is rocky. Love is solid.

17. Infatuation is delusional. Love is real.

18. Infatuation follows a timeline. Love is timeless.

19. Infatuation has unrealistic expectations. Love has realistic standards.

20. Infatuation is childish. Love is mature.

21. Infatuation grows with desire. Love grows with friendship.

22. Infatuation stems from insecurity. Love stems from self-assurance.

23. Infatuation makes you vengeful. Love makes you a better person.

24. Infatuation makes you forget you have a life. Love is integrated with yours.

25. Infatuation can leave unannounced. Love provides explanations.

26. Infatuation is never content with one person. Love is monogamous.

27. Infatuation is undefined. Love is exclusive.

28. Infatuation is loud. Love is quiet.

29. Infatuation can be self-destructive. Love can heal you.

30. Infatuation thinks love should be perfect. Love knows it's not but it doesn't matter.

6

17 Struggles You Go Through When You Are Extremely Guarded Yet Hopelessly Romantic

1. You can have crushes that last for months or years just because you are not willing to initiate contact or make the first move even though you keep thinking about them…a lot.

2. If the person you like approaches you, you will not show any kind of excitement which may come off as 'not interested' but the truth is you are actually quite interested, you just don't know how to handle the first few encounters very well.

3. On dates, you usually do the listening because you want to divert the attention from talking about you as long as you possibly can, despite the fact that you want to open up to them and tell them a lot of things about yourself–including how romantic you really are.

4. You never believe the compliments you get. You always think they are delusive, not genuine or that there is another motive behind it, however, you keep the compliments you want to say to yourself or even say too little because you are not sure how the person will take it.

5. You have so many unsent texts and emails sitting in your inbox since you never had the audacity to send them because of how 'sappy' they were.

6. The moment someone shows interest in you, you will find a reason why it won't work, on the other hand, you envision how lovely it would be if you two were together walking in the park, talking about life.

7. You will keep a fair amount of physical distance at first but you will wonder how the touch of their hands feels like.

8. You will have vulnerable moments and you will think of calling the one you like, but you will end up talking to your best friend instead.

9. You don't trust easily; but deep inside, you want to let the person know exactly why you don't but you also don't want to push them away.

10. You will struggle to make eye contact; you don't want them to know how into them you really are. So you always try to look away.

11. You get cold feet whenever something sounds too good to be true; you think the mask will come off and the real heart breaker will come out, but you also wonder if maybe you are the exception to the rule.

12. You wish you could let anyone you're into talk to your best friend so they can explain to them that there is a very lovable person underneath this mask of ice.

13. You will miss them in several occasions and you will wish they were there with you, but you will never let them know that.

14. When you decide to reach out, you will keep it as short and shallow as possible. "Hi. How are you? Hope all is well." But what you really want to say "Hi. I miss you. I really want to see you."

15. As much as you enjoy coffee dates, what you really want is a whole day full of activities ending with a heart to heart conversation really late at night.

16. You tend to buy things for the people you like but never give it to them because you don't want them to think you are too attached too soon.

17. The truth is, the more romantic you are the more guarded you will be, because you know that if you decide to let someone in, you will go all out and the last time you gave your heart to someone–it got broken, so you keep guarding your heart until you find the person who truly wants to peel off all your layers.

7

30 Crucial Yet Simple Tips For Making Love Last

I was inspired by an article I read recently about a couple sharing their secrets to a successful marriage after being together for over 50 years. It made me wonder what makes a relationship last and how to keep loving someone for decades. I consulted a few happily married couples and I realized it's not as hard as we think it is. It's all in the details.

1. Be honest with each other about your feelings, your needs and your own personal reflections.

2. Be kind to one another. Kind with your words, kind in your actions and kind with your heart.

3. Tell each other *everything*. Secrets, silly things, embarrassing stories, childhood memories and future dreams.

4. Admit your mistakes and put your ego aside. Mistakes can make the relationship stronger once you sincerely admit them and realize that you were wrong.

5. Be each other's biggest fans. Cheer each other on the small things like cooking a great meal and the big things like getting a promotion.

6. Maintain the respect no matter how long you've been together. Respect is the fuel that keeps the relationship going, never lose it.

7. Let go of the little things that bother you. As long as it doesn't take away from your relationship, let it go.

8. Don't expect perfection and don't try to be perfect. Embrace each other for who you truly are and focus on the good qualities you both admire about each other.

9. Find things to laugh about. Movies, old stories, old home videos. Release more dopamine together.

10. Don't lose the passion in the bedroom. Keep it hot, passionate and *innovative.*

11. Never stop appreciating each other for the small things you do and don't take them for granted.

12. Do something special for them every now and then. Plan an exotic vacation, or make a scrapbook of all your memories together. Find ways to let them know how much they mean to you.

13. Be playful. Go to theme parks, karaoke bars and water slides. Keep your heart beating and your free spirit alive.

14. Don't be afraid to show your vulnerability. It will always be part of who you are and you shouldn't be scared to show your partner how much you love them or how soft they make you.

15. Give a little more. Try to give without expecting anything in return. It's not a business trade, it's a relationship.

16. Be each other's reality checks. Be honest about your flaws and setbacks too, tell them the hard things they need to hear sometimes.

17. Treat them like your best friend. You don't hold grudges or give your best friend a hard time. Adopt the same mantra with your partner and you will be amazed at how much easier the relationship will be.

18. Remember the tiny details. Remember what makes them *happy* and what makes them smile and find ways to bring those moments back.

19. Hold hands and cuddle. Nothing beats the classic hand holding and cuddling when it comes to deepening your emotional bond and feeling the real connection between you two.

20. Have a lot of patience with each other. Especially during tough times. Most of the time we let our bad mood out on the people we love the most. Don't take it personally and try to understand where your partner is coming from.

21. Always put each other first. Check in with your partner before doing something selfish or something you know your partner is not a big fan of.

22. Never stop working on *yourself*. The happier you are with yourself, the happier you will make your partner.

23. Give each other the space you need. We all need some time to recharge our batteries to nurture ourselves so we can be able to take care of others.

24. Get involved in their job. Not literally but know what they do, know the latest updates in their company, know their upcoming deadlines and projects. When you are aware of what's happening in their other life, you will be able to offer the right kind of support.

25. Recreate romantic moments. First dates, first kisses, first time you said I love you. Celebrate the beautiful memories by reliving them.

26. Get lost together. In a foreign country, on a new adventure or on a cruise. Go somewhere where no one knows your name.

27. Buy things for each other and send your partner anything that reminds you of them.

28. Enjoy the silence. Don't try to fill your time together with noise. Get comfortable with just being silent together and feel the true definition of comfort.

29. Engage them with your family. Let them be part of it–the good, the bad and the ugly.

30. Choose each other. Keep *choosing* to love each other and be together every single day.

8

I Want To Waste My Days With You

I want to waste my days with you, talking about life, telling each other stories about our past and our wishes for the future. I want to waste my mornings with you, catching you up on years and years of untold stories, family secrets, friends drama and a long list of heartbreaks. *I want to waste my words on you.*

I want to waste my afternoons with you, driving ourselves to unfamiliar places; exploring the city as we listen to your favorite songs and as you listen to my favorite lyrics and as we replay our favorite songs over and over again. I want us to go to museums, galleries, festivals, concerts and anything we come cross. *I want to waste my money on you.*

I want to waste my evenings with you, walking by the lake, watching the sunset, remembering the times when we didn't think the sun will ever shine, when we were blinded by our own darkness and how we came to find the light. *I want to shine my light on you.*

I want to waste my nights with you. I want to dance with you under the moonlight and I want to take you to all my favorite restaurants and bars and show you my favorite spots. Where I go when I need to think, where I go when I need to be alone, and where I go when I want to hide from the world. *I want to waste my secrets on you.*

I want to waste my heart on you. I want to spoil you and buy you gifts you don't need. I want to help you love the parts of you that you gravely hate. I want to heal the scars that life left on you and I want to keep giving you all I've got – *profusely* and *lavishly. I want to waste my love on you.*

I want to waste my sleep with you. I want to stay up looking at you when I can barely open my eyes. I want to stay up listening to you when I can't utter a word. I want you to be the reason why I couldn't wake up in the morning and I want you to be the reason for my incurable insomnia. *I want to waste my sleepless nights on you.*

I want to waste the best years of my life with you. Traveling, exploring the world, exploring adulthood, exploring life and watching ourselves grow through life. I want to spend my years in your arms that feel like home. *I want to waste the best years of my life making memories with you.*

I want to waste my time with you. I want every moment to be filled with something of you. I want time to fly with you, I want time to pass me by with you, or maybe *I want time to stop with you.*

I guess what I am trying to say is **I don't want to waste a minute unless I am wasting it away with you.**

9

10 Reasons Why Dating A Girl With A Big Heart Will Mend Yours

Even though looks can be the first thing that attracts you to a woman, it's her heart that keeps you. A big heart is hard to find, but unlike looks, it lasts forever. It's forever young and full of love. The girl with a big heart will make you believe in love again.

1. She will never run out of love. Her love overflows more and more as time goes by, she is ready to pour her love on those she really cares about. Her heart thrives on giving love more than receiving it. Her love is deep, meaningful and pure. She will definitely love you with *all* her heart.

2. She appreciates the small things. It won't take a lot to make her happy. A simple 'have a good day!' or 'good morning' is all you need to make her smile.

3. She is sincere. When she asks you questions about your work, your family or your life, she really wants to know – she is not asking because she's obliged to. She is genuinely interested in your life and in what makes you happy.

4. She will feel your joy and your pain as if it was hers.

When you're happy and celebrating, she will throw you the biggest and happiest party and when you're sad, she will be suffering for you, she doesn't want to see you upset or hurt and she will do whatever it takes to make you feel better. She will truly be there for you *in sickness and in health.*

5. She sees the best in you. She sees who you really are and who you can be and she will always believe in you. The girl with the big heart will make you want to be a better person. You will start seeing yourself the way she sees you.

6. She will be your parents' favorite. Your parents will love her because they will see how much she cares about you and how much she loves you. You will never have to worry about your mom not liking her, she has a nurturing nature that your mom will fall in love with.

7. She forgives easily. The bigger her heart, the more forgiving she will be. She is not going to hold grudges or engage in any passive aggressive behavior, she will simply let things go. You don't have to sweat the small stuff; she doesn't take them seriously anyway.

8. She is extremely honest. She is candid and straight-forward. You don't have to wonder if she is lying to you or if you should trust her. She will put your trust issues to rest and will introduce to loyalty, integrity and *easy* communication.

9. She is compassionate. You don't have to pretend to be someone else around her. If you feel like you want to cry or let your guard down or open up about your past, she won't judge you or love you any less. Her kind heart accepts all parts of you equally, the dark and muddy and the bright and shiny. She's the one you could really be yourself with – *unapologetically.*

10. She will be a fantastic mother. Her heart always has room for more love, that's why if you ever decide to have kids with her, you can guarantee that they are in the best hands and they will have a warm and loving *home.* Love has a way of spreading and it will definitely fill up every corner of your home.

10

This Is How I Want You To Remember Me

I want you to remember me when the world gets cold, when you can't catch your breath from the weight of the burdens and chores that you are carrying on your shoulders. I want you to remember my warmth and how it took some of the weight away.

I want you to remember me when you are feeling down and anxious, when you can't see the light at the end of the tunnel. I want you to remember my naïve optimism and the paragraphs I used to send you about how wonderful life could be and how wonderful you are. I want you to remember how unrealistic I was but it *somehow* made you feel better.

I want you to remember me when you are doubting yourself, when you are unsure if you can achieve something. I want you to remember how I believed in you and the potential I saw in you. I want you to remember that I said you were destined for greatness. I want you to remember that I always thought you were strong and determined.

I want you to remember me when you are dancing, I want you to remember how much I loved to dance and how I would force you to keep up with me. I want you to remember how you acted like you hated it but you secretly loved it. *I want you to remember that our short time together was exactly like a dance; liberating, intimate, fun and hypnotic.*

I want you to remember me when you are walking alone in the city, when it's quiet at night. I want you to remember the conversations we had in every corner and the laughter that echoed between the walls. I want you to remember how easy it was to open up to each other and how it felt like we are the only two people in the world who could truly understand each other. I want you to remember the way we looked at each other and how the moon was looking at us – *witnessing the birth of a new love story.*

I want you to remember me when you are taking pictures, and how I forced you to take too many of them. I want you to remember the goofy faces and the silly poses and the awkward smiles, and I want you to remember the sweet ones, the ones that captured the beautiful memories, the ones that captured the unforgettable experiences we had together. I want you to remember the smile on my face when I was next to you and the moment we both knew this was something special.

I want you to remember me when you read a poem, I want you to remember my words; how they touched you, how they made you feel, how they described you when you couldn't even describe yourself and how they built you up when you were tearing yourself down. I want you to remember how my words brought you closer and how they made you fall in love with me. I want you to remember how my sentences completed yours and how my words filled up your silence and slowly pulled you away from your solitude.

I want you to remember me and smile. I want you to remember me and feel like it wasn't one of those sad endings. I want you to remember that even the ending was sweet. That the ending was inevitable but it was worth it. I want you to remember that for the first time you don't have to force yourself to forget someone, you don't have to forget about your feelings or your memories. That my name doesn't hurt when you hear it, that my pictures don't make you cringe when you see them. I want you to remember me as the first person that proved to you that lost love is not completely lost, that we sometimes meet wonderful people who are not meant to stay forever and that some people will always hold a special place in our hearts because we want to *keep* them there.

This is how I want you to remember me, because this is exactly how I remember you.

Part 2

Letting Go and Moving On

There are far better things ahead than any we leave behind.
– C.S Lewis

11

The Art of Letting Go

Letting go is really hard, especially when you have to let go of something you really want, whether it's a great opportunity, someone you really liked or loved or even any expectations you had about something. I don't think anyone knows how to completely let go or not fall back from time to time if they do, but there are definitely ways to make it easier for you to let go when you relentlessly don't want to let go.

What is destined will reach you, even if it be underneath two mountains. What is not destined, will not reach you, even if it be between your two lips.
—Proverb

Anything that feels forced or harder than it should be or causes you pain and distress is not meant for you. Having this mentality or faith will help you overcome the reluctance that comes with making a decision of whether or not you should let go. Things that are meant for you have a way of flowing smoothly into your life. The more you fight for something that is not meant for you, the more it will fight you. You may get what you want in the end, but it may not last and you may not feel at ease with it. The beauty of things that are meant for you is that they just happen; against all odds. We are just programmed to *complicate* life sometimes.

The only thing more unthinkable than leaving was staying; the only thing more impossible than staying was leaving.
—Elizabeth Gilbert

Letting go is really painful when you feel "stuck" and it can sometimes seem impossible to do, but the truth is if you reach this point, it means that you've been trying so hard to make this thing work in your favor, or reach your goal, and it sometimes feel like we've tried so hard or come a long way that if we let go now, it will feel like a waste of time given the time and effort we invested in it. But nothing is a waste of time, even if it feels like it is, we are here to make mistakes and learn lessons to grow as individuals, if we keep holding on to toxic situations or toxic people because we've already done too much or it's too late to change things, we are only setting ourselves up for a miserable life. There is power in letting go, a power that brings more peace and serenity than being stuck in situations that make your heart a bit heavier each and every day.

If you're brave enough to say goodbye, life will reward you with a new hello.
—Paulo Coelho

This outlook really helps you move on and let go faster. Same notion that when one door closes another opens. Life opens new doors for you all the time; imagine you are a key to multiple doors and you just think you can only open one door. We have so much potential, so many talents, so many kind things to give back to the world. We have so many keys to open so many doors. When you leave one door behind and lock that door, you will be surprised by the number of doors that were waiting to be open by you and only you. Some endings are not bad; sometimes they are not even endings – just bridges to new beginnings.

I think part of the reason we hold on to something so tight is because we fear something so great won't happen twice.
—Anonymous

Here's another reason why we hold on to things or people longer than we should. We convince ourselves that good things won't happen twice; we will not be able to find someone who is that great again or who makes us feel this way again. Or we won't be able to find a job like that again, or something we are that passionate about again. The truth is, you will always find something or someone that makes you feel this way again, new passions will emerge and good things will happen twice and as many times as they want, and will probably be a better and more convenient fit for you. If you look back at your life, you will find yourself laughing at certain situations when you thought you would never move on from someone, or how you held on to something so tightly only to realize later that it was wrong for you. Great things happen to us all the time in different shapes or forms; we just like to focus on the things that are not so great. Holding on to something out of fear that it will never happen again, is the definition of fear. We have to be fearless in letting go.

See it for what is, not what you want it to be.
—*Anonymous*

The truth is if you reach a point where letting go is the only option, it usually means that this thing or someone already let you go. You are trying to stay in a place where you are not welcome anymore. The mind has a funny of way of tricking us into believing certain things to make it less painful for us, or put it in a way that doesn't really hurt our pride or break our heart, but we have to look at it the way it is, the way it is being portrayed to us, not the way we want to see it. This is not an optical illusion, this is reality, and in reality what you see is what you get. If an opportunity passed you by, it didn't really want to stop at your station, if someone let you go, they didn't really want to stay, if someone else got what you were praying for, this blessing was not written for you to begin with and you will be blessed in another way. As you keep learning the art of letting go, let go of your fear, of your past, of your mistakes, of your insecurities, of your failures, of your self-doubt. Forgive yourself enough to let go of the parts of you that dim your light.

12

When You Fall In Love With Mr. Maybe Instead Of Mr. Right

Once upon a time, I fell in love with a good man, he was smart, ambitious, polite, handsome and charming. It was hard not to fall head over heels for him, I will call him Mr. Maybe. During that time, I tried convincing myself that he was doing all he could do to love me and was trying to give it his all, but I knew I was lying to myself because I always felt something was missing, like he could do more or give more but something was just impeding him from doing so.

For the longest time I made excuses for him, until I just decided that I was done with Mr. Maybe and all his maybes.

Let me tell you exactly what it feels like to fall in love with Mr. Maybe:

"Maybe" he is free at 10 PM to call you and chat for a bit.

"Maybe" he is attending your friend's wedding, or your cousin's birthday or your job promotion celebration.

"Maybe" he is listening to you when you are talking about a personal issue.

"Maybe" he supports your dreams and passions but doesn't think it is a good idea to drop everything and pursue them.

"Maybe" he really is too busy.

"Maybe" he cares but doesn't know how to show it.

"Maybe" he is just stressed out at work and that is why he hasn't been making any effort.

"Maybe" he is so focused on his career and doesn't want a relationship to distract him.

"Maybe" he needs you in his life, but he is emotionally unavailable.

"Maybe" he didn't mean to ignore you when you told him you miss him.

"Maybe" he needs space because he is just overwhelmed with work and his family issues.

"Maybe" he didn't hear you when you said you loved him that night.

"Maybe" he didn't mean to let go of your hand when you were crossing the street.

"Maybe" he got wrapped up in something that he forgot to call you back.

"Maybe" he really didn't like your profile picture, or your article or your status update.

"Maybe" he loves you but he has been hurt before.

"Maybe" he doesn't know how to be loved because he isn't used to receiving that kind of love.

"Maybe" he is being distant because he is intimidated by your love for him.

"Maybe" he is just not ready.

The list of Mr. Maybe's "maybes" can go on forever, these are just a few examples of how love can blind people into settling for "maybes" when they know better, and they know that "maybe" is just another word for not really that into it, or you are just not that important to me to try harder. Mr. Maybe and I remained good friends for some reason. He once asked me if I will ever invite him to my wedding, I would just like him to know that the day I get married, I will be marrying the man who was sure of all his "maybes".

I will be marrying the man who knew that when it comes to me, there should be no "maybes". I will be marrying the man who has never been sure of anything more than this, more than me, more than wanting to spend the rest of his life with me. But to answer his question, will he get an invite to my wedding? *Maybe.*

13

This Is Why You Shouldn't Wait For Someone To Make Up Their Mind

I used to think that waiting for someone you love to be ready is the ultimate form of flattery and the ideal declaration of love.

It's how all epic love stories unfold and those who waited are finally rewarded for their patience when their lover comes back to them, then I had a very simple epiphany- the most epic love stories start when two people decide they like each other, they want to be with each other and they want to make the relationship work. Love is not always going to be easy and there will always be compromises, but having to wait for someone for months or years to finally decide to give you a chance should not be one of them.

Admit it, you don't know what you are waiting for. Are you waiting for a declaration of love? Are you waiting for someone to change? Are you waiting for someone to recognize how loyal and patient you are? Are you waiting for a sign? Whatever it is you are waiting for should not keep you waiting if it's truly worth it and you should always ask yourself if you are waiting for something that may never happen.

Waiting for someone means that you are okay with that person treating you like you are not important or that you don't deserve their time.

Waiting for someone means that you don't value yourself enough to realize that if someone cares enough, they will not keep you waiting or wondering. You are choosing to blind your own eyes from seeing the truth that will eventually blindside you.

Waiting for someone is not a sign of strength or loyalty, it's a sign of denial and ignoring what you already know to be true. You will continue putting them on a pedestal they don't even know they're on, you will continue investing your all on nothing.

Waiting for someone means that you are pouring salt on your own cuts and acting like it doesn't burn. It means that you have agreed to be the person they "settle" for after exploring all other options. It means that you are surrendering yourself to rejection over and over again and acting like it's the natural process of waiting.

Waiting for someone means you are pushing away people who are willing to give what you are waiting for and they are willing to give it to you *immediately*. It means you are telling the whole world that you do not deserve the respect and love that you give others, that you are willing to compromise the most precious parts of yourself for someone who doesn't even try to give a little bit more.

As much as you deserve to be rewarded for your patience and as much as you deserve someone who comes back and finally claims you, this is not always the case. You shouldn't set aside yourself for anyone else, because when you lose a person for whatever reason you are going to realize that you are on your own, and that you waited months or years for someone who didn't end up fulfilling the prophecy you created for them. Sometimes patience is a waste of time.

If you must wait; wait to be chosen every day, wait to be reminded that you are special, wait to be loved in the way that you constantly love, wait to be taken seriously and wait for someone who doesn't keep you waiting, because you know that you deserve better than waiting around for someone to make up their mind.

14

Why Love Alone Is Never Enough

The past year I've witnessed more breakups than any other year. Breakups I didn't see coming, breakups the couple involved didn't see coming. The common factor in most of these breakups was that the love was still very much there, strongly present, yet it wasn't enough to keep the relationship going. I fought for the idea that love conquers all, that love makes anything work, even the hardest of relationships. But then I realized that love alone is not enough. It is the pillar you build the relationship on, but it is not the fuel that keeps it going.

You can love someone who is not right for you.

You can truly love someone but they still won't be right for you. You can be either too similar or too different to the point that you can't really meet half-way. You both can be too stubborn to admit it, and even more stubborn to end the relationship. Eventually though, loving someone who is not right for you can feel like tug of war, you keep pulling and pulling until someone slips away.

You can love someone but the timing won't be right.

You can do whatever it takes to make it work, but one of you may still not be ready to take the next step. One of you may be tired of waiting for the next step. One of you may get a big shot at a dream job and abandon everything else. One of you may just be starting grad school and want to solely focus on their education. Whatever the reason may be, it's hard to schedule a meeting when your life timetables are not aligning.

You can love someone but the parents can get in the way.

Even though it's 2016 and our generation is more independent than ever, parents still have a say one way or another. You can be in love with each other, but if her dad is not a big fan or his mom is not a big fan, the relationship is doomed. A relationship that doesn't have the parents' blessing is usually *not* blessed. Curse the stars, curse the universe, it's hard to fight the parental force once it gets a hold of you.

You can love someone who needs help.

You can be in love with someone who needs help, and I mean clinical help. We are all crazy in our own way, but some people truly need therapy, and until they fix themselves, you can't really fix them. **You can try to help, you can be supportive, you can be the most loving and nurturing person out there, but you still won't be their remedy.** And they can love with all they've got, but because they're their own worst enemy, or because they are damaged, they will most likely destroy the relationship along the way. It's what they know, it's what they understand, and until they get help, there is no way the relationship will survive.

You can love someone that you can't keep up with.

You can love someone but you fight 50 times a day. You can love someone who is always working. You can love someone who is always on their phone. You can love someone who can't open up about their feelings. You can love someone who changes their mind like they change their outfits. **While you may think that love can outdo all of the above, sometimes it can't.** Sometimes it gets exhausting to keep up. It drains you when you can't foretell what kind of person you will have to deal with. It sucks the happiness out of you to know that you are coming up against a brick wall. Love can start to feel like hard work — work you just can't put up with anymore even though you need it, even though you love it.

You can love someone who makes you love yourself a little less.

It's paradoxical and ironic and sadistic that someone can love you to an extent that makes you not love yourself. Love is a drug, and sometimes the high of the drug fizzles out and you are left with anger and anxiety and the need for a fix that is not always obtainable. You can't go without it, but you know it is slowly killing you. Some people love each other so much but there is no understanding, there is no patience, there is no peace, there is no tolerance. The truth of the matter is that love *only* works when it is combined with a bunch of other factors to make it grow; like respect, humility, compatibility and commitment. Relationships based on the feelings of love alone crumble, because love can't stand on its own, and love does not always equal happily ever after.

15

Read This If You Can't Forget Someone Who Has Already Forgotten You

There are two main reasons why we struggle to forget someone: 1) We truly believe they are the one for us. 2) We fear that we will not find anyone better. However, we should all remember two things: 1) If someone *is* the right person for us, they will come back into our lives no matter how far away they drift. 2) You will always be able to find someone better—or, rather, someone just as good who won't forget you.

Feeling forgotten or neglected by someone you care deeply about can be one of the most soul-crushing & excruciating feelings in the world. Instead of forcing yourself to try, in vain, to forget that person, I want you to free yourself to remember them.

Remember them when you are alone at night crying, remember the pain they put you through, remember when you almost lost your breath because of the tears you shed over them, and remember how you had to hide your eyes behind your sunglasses so no one could see them, or see *you*.

Remember them on your birthday, remember how they are actively choosing not to celebrate another year with you, **remember that they are happier celebrating somewhere else, maybe with someone else**. Remember that they want to grow old without you.

Remember them when you are lonely, remember how they once promised not to leave you, remember how they could have turned your loneliness around but they left you staring at all four walls as they found someone else to ease their lonely nights.

Remember them when you attend an engagement party or a wedding, remember that instead of being your plus one, they left you minus one. Remember that they convinced you that you were heading in that direction but suddenly decided to make a U-turn and drove away on their own.

Remember them when your family asks about your relation-ship status, remember how you could have easily avoided that question had they been there to answer it. **Remember that they didn't want to give you an answer or even help you find it.**

Remember them when you are having a blast with your friends, remember that this is how they should've made you feel, but they decided to be strangers. They decided they'd rather treat you like a *stranger* not a friend.

Remember them when you are smiling because someone appreciates you, remember how they didn't and remember how they slowly took that smile away from you. **Remember that they chose to make someone else smile instead.**

Remember them every time you want to forget them, remember that they are not remembering you, and remember that they want you to forget them.

Remember them when you finally get over them, remember them when you see them and no longer recognize them.

16

The Moment I Realized I Was Finally Over You

There was a moment when I thought that no matter what happens I will never get you out of my head, I will never get over you and I will never forget you. I wanted you engraved in my heart and stored in my mind. I wanted to live all those heartbreaking songs and romantic novels through you. I wanted you to be my happy place, but that was before I realized I had a *choice* – a choice to sincerely let you go.

There was a moment when holding on to the thought of you coming back consumed me and made me feel alive. I looked forward to the long-awaited reunion and the most romantic reconciliation story this generation ever witnessed, until I realized I am neglecting what someone has to offer me *now*. Someone with a solid plan and solid actions, someone who doesn't make my love life a fantasy for *"someday."*

There was a moment when I would go back and read your old messages and believe in them all over again, until I realized I was looking at a screen that can't hold my hand and tell me that everything is going to be alright.

There was a moment when I was upset because I didn't hear from you on my birthday, until I realized that even when you attended my birthday, I never really felt your presence. **And every year I grew accustomed to your absence in each milestone in my life.**

There was a moment when I called your friend to ask about you, until I realized you are fine and doing well and don't need me around. And I wondered if this has always been the case and I was just living in the fantasy of you and I.

There was a moment when I broke so many hearts trying to forget you, until I realized that they don't deserve to pay the price of your selfishness or your mistakes and that I have to mend my own heart.

There was a moment when I blamed everyone but you that it didn't work out between us, until I realized I could keep playing the blame game forever but I will still lose.

There was a moment when that heartbreaking song came on and I almost turned the volume up, until I realized that I can just change the station and listen to a different song.

There was a moment when I prayed for you to come back, until I realized that I should pray for someone who never leaves instead.

There was a moment when I almost let someone amazing go because he was not you, until I realized that this is a good thing and it is what I had been asking for – **to never fall in love with someone like you again.**

Now I look at your old texts, listen to these heartbreaking

songs and remember my juvenile fantasy and smile. Smile because they all got me to where I belong. They got me to appreciate a happier place I never thought of. They got me to ask for a lifetime without you. They got me to rethink some of my old beliefs. They got me to find someone better. They got me to love myself and *that* was the moment I realized I was finally over you.

17

10 Unforgettable Lessons You Learn From Dating The Wrong Guy

Don't you wish there was a fast track to Mr. Right? It would save us from a lot of heartbreak and drama. However, Mr. Wrong can also save us from further heartbreak and drama– if we choose to take the lessons he taught us. Here are 10 crucial lessons you learn from dating the wrong guy.

1. Value your time.

When you waste a lot of time with the wrong guy, you learn to value your time in the future and only give it to those who deserve it. Time you could've spent building a strong relationship and getting to know one another. It's easier when you are young to waste more time exploring with someone you don't see a future with but as you get older, your time becomes more important and wrong guys will not value the importance of your time.

2. Trust your gut.

More often than not, your intuition tells you if this guy is going to be serious about you or not, and sometimes you just choose to neglect it waiting for a surprise or a change of heart. You can always tell if a guy is being truthful to you and if he has the right intentions. The wrong guy teaches you how to listen to your gut.

3. No one is busy all the time.

Even though people can be *very* busy and probably are; they still have time to do things for the people they care about, and if they don't, they let them know that and then reschedule. When a guy keeps telling you he is busy–he is lying. Even the busiest of guys will make time for a woman they are really into.

4. Know your boundaries.

The wrong guy teaches you what you can and cannot tolerate. What is acceptable to you and what isn't. It's normal to sub-consciously compromise our standards when we really like someone but sometimes it breaks the relationship rather than mend it. The wrong guy helps you tap into your subconscious and identify how far you are willing to go and if you are being taken for granted.

5. The difference between circumstances and excuses.

The wrong guy helps you distinguish between someone who can't do something because they absolutely *can't* or someone who can't do something because they don't *want* to. The wrong guy comes up with excuses for all the things he could've easily done but chose not to. He is the perfect archetype for someone who simply doesn't want to make an effort.

6. Words are beautiful but they are not enough.

The wrong guy can say all the right things and do all the wrong things, and sometimes you will believe everything he says and wait for it to come to life; only to realize that it just won't happen. The wrong guy will buy himself time by saying things he doesn't mean, which will teach you to just wait for actions instead of being hung up on lies or words blurted out on the spur of the moment.

7. What you are truly looking for.

Sometimes you think you want a certain type of guy only to realize that this type is actually not compatible with you and will not be able to give you the connection you desire. Dating the wrong guys teaches you exactly what you are looking for. You no longer date someone because they *"look good on paper,"* you date them because you think you two can connect on a deeper level and they respect who you really are.

8. The kind of guys you need to steer clear of.

The wrong guy teaches you exactly the type of guys you should beware of and how to avoid them. You have a better idea of where these guys hang out and how they act and you will be able to spot them before you get emotionally attached. A guy usually shows his true colors early on, you just need to know what to look for.

9. A relationship should make you happy.

Even though happiness is a broad and vague term, a relationship should bring you *joy* and comfort more than anything else. It definitely shouldn't leave you sad and angry most of the time. The wrong guy teaches you that if all you do is argue and fight or if the good moments are sporadic, then it is time to walk away. This is not how a healthy relationship operates.

10. What you *deserve*.

The most important lesson you learn is what you deserve and how you should be treated, when to walk away from someone who is not right for you and when to let go of someone who does not meet your standards. You know your worth and you know that you want a relationship that makes you grow and a relationship that is worth your time, effort and *heart*.

18

To The One Who Was Not 'The One'

They say that if a man is not ready for commitment, even if you bring him all the ladies in the world and hand it to him on a silver platter, he still will not commit. They also say that if a man really values you and doesn't want to lose you, he will do everything he can to keep you, because that is the real challenge, the challenge is not getting someone –the challenge is *keeping* them.

I was trying to find a happy medium between two paradoxical facts, so I was giving you your time but at the same time I wanted *more* from you. We had good times, we laughed, we had intimate conversations, and we had a very strong connection, but you also had that with many other women, and I had that with many other men. Sometimes I felt we acted more like friends than lovers but isn't that a *good* thing? Either way I wanted to *make this work*. I was tired of failed relationships, I was tired of meaningless flings, I was tired of being lonely, I was just tired and you gave me something to fight for.
You come to understand that all you ever want is to be loved a little more, and understood a little better, and sometimes you can't just keep these two truths under wraps.

I fought for you and for the relationship to work, but later on I realized that if I continue fighting, I will be fighting myself, because in the soundless moments that I refrained from everyone and thought about this relationship, that little voice inside my head told me that **it's not what you want, it's not how it should be, you are not happy,** and when I paused and reflected, I was the only one fighting, while you were *trying.*

I think the older you get, you look for those who can comfort you and be there for you as opposed to someone you can have fun with or just kill time with. You want security, knowing that when everyone walks out of your life, that person will walk in, and I never felt that, I felt that you were in the front line of people who are constantly disappointing me. **So I left, and I may have looked back a couple of times, but it was nothing more than pure nostalgia.**

I guess this is what's funny about relationships, you think you want something out of a specific relationship only to realize that you want something totally different.

I don't know if it's because you get to know yourself better, or because in the darkest of moments, when you are alone in bed thinking about the meaning of life, you come to understand that **all you ever want is to be loved a little more, and understood a little better, and sometimes you can't just keep these two truths under wraps** and when you unravel them, you want to make sure that your partner will embrace them instead of running away.

You were always "busy" doing other stuff; sometimes

absolutely *nothing*, but you always chose "busy" over me, and eventually I chose me over "busy" and started giving more time to those who made time for me. **Why do we always remember those who were always there for us when we find no one else? Why can't we just value their presence without having to feel their absence?**

When I saw how amazing you were to your friends, I realized that you are capable of being a giving & generous man–just not with *me*. How do you explain that? I don't know. Maybe this where the whole *'not meant to be'* thing comes into play. We just didn't bring out the best in each other. Why? *Because we weren't meant to be.*

Thank you for teaching me that no matter how hard I try to change myself to please someone, they can still reject me.

So I guess I thank you for paving the way for me to know who I should be with, the kind of man I should look for, and what I want out of a relationship. Thank you for teaching me that no matter how hard I try to change myself to please someone, they can still reject me.

Thank you for making me embrace my core and stop changing myself for a relationship that does not go the distance. Thank you for reminding me that people can say we are so *'perfect'* together, and then say *'we saw it coming'* when it's over. I learned not to listen to them anymore.

Thank you for making me realize how dangerous infatuation can be, we soon find ourselves doing things we never thought we would, so blinded by the *very* obvious facts, and clinging to strings of false hope. Sometimes you ask yourself what was I thinking? The answer is *you weren't*.

It wasn't easy getting over you, attachment is a double-edged sword, but I learned that in relationships **it's better to break your own heart and save yourself from falling apart**. Thank you for making me aware of the lines we shouldn't cross in relationships, and how *blurry* these lines can be when you're in love. Thank you for bringing me one step closer to '*the one*.'

19

What It Feels Like To Get Over Someone You Never Thought You Would

I don't know how or when it happens but it does, one morning you wake up and you don't look at your phone waiting for a text or a call. You make plans without considering whether he'll like it or not and you finally tell everyone you no longer think about him.

It feels like getting your memory back long after you've lost it. You slowly begin to remember what it feels like to live lightly without the heavy weight on your shoulders or your heart. You remember what it feels like to laugh uncontrollably with your friends; laughter that's not followed by a tinge of sadness. You remember what it feels like to actually talk to and see other people without missing him. You remember that your life was waiting for you and you chose to get locked away from it all.

It feels like the first day you got your car, when all you wanted to do was take it and drive everywhere, listen to your favorite songs and pick up your friends. You are ready to take yourself and go everywhere to make up for the times when you couldn't even *hit the brakes*. You gladly enjoy the ride and the road and dance in your car. You want to smile at strangers, go to your favorite restaurants and shop at all your favorite stores. You finally recall your love for driving after being stuck on a dead-end road.

It feels like finishing a book you were reading, you took your notes, learned the lessons and understood the main message behind the book. Now it's time to find a new book to read. It's time to find new chapters and new pages to turn, time to find new lessons and new notes to take. It's time to find different endings to the same old stories.

It feels like the pieces of you are coming back together again, you look at his pictures and it no longer hurts, you hear his name and it no longer matters, you pass by his apartment and it no longer makes you feel empty, you go to his favorite bar and he no longer crosses your mind, you see him and you can finally think of him as part of your *past* – not your present or your future.

Maybe some stories are meant to end this way – without closures, without explanations, without answers. Maybe some stories are meant to be left alone, maybe some stories are not meant to be revisited. Maybe some things are meant to be chaotic and scattered and not meant to be restored. Maybe some memories are meant to be forgotten and washed away, maybe we are meant to drown before we can truly learn how to swim.

20

To My Hardest Goodbye

All my life
you were always on my mind
with all its ups and downs
you were there for the whole ride

Your smile made me smile
and your words kept me going
your touch kept me safe
and your love kept me growing

Your calm held back my storms
and your wisdom cured my insanity
your patience made me stronger
and your perspective gave me clarity

Although you were all I had
life continues to get in the way
I guess timing is not our friend
sadly, I have to walk away

Because I can't have it both ways
I have to let you go
I need to go and find myself
So I can one day be like *you*

It's going be hard saying goodbye

and even harder watching you leave
it is going to hurt when you're not around
but you'll always be why I *believe*

I'm going to miss you so much
I hope fate doesn't make this the end
you will always be in my heart
you will always be my best friend

As I pray for us once more
your memory is what I'll keep
I will think of you one last time
And then I'm off to sleep.

21

I Still Wonder About You

I still wonder about you, a lot more than I should, and a lot more than I reveal. After all we've been through, it's hard for me to reach out to you because I know—the whole world knows—that we will never be what I wanted us to be. Still, I wonder about *you*.

I wonder if you remember all the details of the first time you told me you had feelings for me, and how happy I was. When I thought all my prayers were being answered through you, that you were finally here to rescue me from all those failed relationships and meaningless flings.

I wonder if you still listen to that song I told you about, and if you think of me every time it comes on, and I wonder how it makes you feel.

I wonder if Adele makes you think of me.

I wonder if you miss talking to me after a long, hard day at work, and if you still think I can make you smile when you are tired.

I wonder if you know that I enjoyed every moment with you more than I enjoyed my entire life.

I wonder if you think of me as someone who is so close yet so far away.

I wonder if you are aware that so many words were left unsaid between us, and I wonder if you are curious to find out what they were.

I wonder if you read what I write, and I wonder if you smile when you read between the lines.

I wonder if I made it hard for you to sleep at night.

I wonder if you figured out that I needed to love myself the way I loved you, and that I needed to see myself the way I saw you.

I wonder if you like who I am becoming and I wonder if you will ever try to find out why I disappeared.

I wonder if you knew how far I was willing to go to make you happy.

I wonder if you worry that I might have met someone else.

I wonder if you met someone else yourself, and I wonder if she will ever look at you the way I did, and if she will listen to you even when you are quiet. You were always quiet.

I wonder if you are still having issues with your dad, and I wonder if there is someone there to reassure you that you are doing just fine and that you need to stop being so hard on yourself. You were always so hard on yourself.

I wonder if you still tell bad jokes, and if you miss the way I laughed at them, or if you miss my "obnoxious but lovable" laugh.

I wonder what comes to your mind when you hear my name and if it still means anything to you.

I wonder even though there is no point in wondering.

I wonder even though I know we are not right for each other.

I wonder because deep down inside, I know you wonder too.

22

10 Reasons Why Most Men Can't Handle A Deep Woman

The deeper you are, the harder it becomes for you to find someone who wants to have a relationships with you. You can go out on a lot of dates but at some point the relationship fails to progress any further and that is mainly because of the intensity of your depth. Not every man is strong enough to handle a deep woman. Here's why.

1. A deep woman asks deep questions.

A deep woman will probe further into your life and ask questions that you may not be prepared to answer. Even on the first date, she will dig deeper and ask personal and philosophical questions – she will never enjoy a shallow conversation.

2. A deep woman is honest.

Too honest – often blunt. A deep woman takes her integrity seriously and one thing she believes in is honesty. If you ask her anything, she will tell you the truth and she expects the same from you.

3. A deep woman knows what she wants.

Or *who* she wants. A deep woman knows right away if she likes you and doesn't need to date around or explore her other options to be sure of her feelings. Her heart only beats for a special few people and she knows them right away.

4. A deep woman wants a deep relationship.

She wants long conversations about your life, she wants to hear stories about your past, she wants to understand your pain and she wants to add value to your life. She wants a real relationship that goes beyond going out and having fun.

5. A deep woman is not afraid of intimacy.

She is not afraid of getting closer or risking getting hurt in the process. She doesn't think it will entrap her freedom or make her vulnerable. Her depth and intimacy go hand in hand and she will always cherish the beauty of intimacy in relationships.

6. A deep woman sees through you.

She can see who you really are and what makes you vulnerable. She is not the one to hold back from pointing out what she sees in you or how well she can read you. Even though it makes you uncomfortable, she wants you to know that she understands you and that you can be yourself around her.

7. A deep woman craves consistency.

She gets turned off by inconsistency or flaky behavior. She desires a strong connection and a solid bond and she knows that consistency is the foundation of that bond. A deep woman will not participate in the dating games.

8. A deep woman is intense.

She may be slightly intimidating because she brings intensity to everything she does. Her emotions are intense and so are her thoughts. She will never be indifferent about things that matter to her – not everyone is strong enough to handle her intensity.

9. A deep woman only knows how to love deeply.

If you can't love her deeply, she will walk away. She doesn't know how to casually date someone she's really into or be friends with someone she has feelings for. A deep woman knows when someone can't meet her halfway and she will slowly detach herself from anyone who is not willing to give her the deep love she is looking for.

10. A deep woman won't wait for you.

She will not wait for you to make up your mind or watch you be hesitant about her. She is strong and passionate and will not waste her emotions on someone who doesn't appreciate their depth. Even though she is looking for a special kind of love, a deep woman is not afraid of being on her own.

23

This Is Why You Suddenly Miss Me

Because I never lied to you.

I never told you I was someone else, I never evaded your questions, I never said anything I didn't mean. I was always honest with you about everything and you never had to worry about me being deceitful because you actually *trusted* me.

Because I never misled you.

I never told you I was ready when I wasn't, I never promised you something I didn't fulfill. I never talked about a future I didn't see, and I never played with your heart or your mind. You knew that my words will be followed by actions and you knew that I always kept my word with you.

Because I was there for you.

For the late night calls, for the big work events, for the family drama, for the boring days and the lonely nights. I was there for the hard conversations and for the silence. I was always there whenever you needed me and you didn't have to even ask for it.

Because I made you laugh.

When you were tired or moody, I would make you laugh. I would make you laugh with me and at me, and I laughed with you. Even if I was sad, I would still make you laugh.

Because I understood you.

I understood your murky eyes, your forged smile, the way your body moves when you're agitated and the way it moves when you're relaxed. I understood the calm before the storm, I understood your need for space. I understood you and I didn't need explanations.

Because I was your sweet escape.

I was your sweet distraction from your gloomy world. I was the cute text in the middle of a busy work day. I was the reassuring morning call before a big presentation, I was the chill nights, I was the unwinding in bed doing nothing days, I was the smile you needed to keep your sanity.

Because I forgave you.

I forgave your negligence, your selfishness, your isolation, your harsh words and the times you failed to understand me. I forgave you for the things you weren't sorry for and I forgave you for all the things you could've done but chose not to. I truly forgave you.

Because I accepted you.

For who you really were, for the person you were behind the mask that everyone seemed to buy. I accepted your darkness, your flaws, your weaknesses and your insecurities. I accepted you wholeheartedly; even when you were *unacceptable*, I accepted you.

Because I moved on.

I am no longer yours, you can't reach me anymore, you can't call me in the middle of the night, you can't take me to dinner, you can't talk to me when you have a problem, and you can't depend on me to *fix* you anymore. You miss me because you know I will find someone better.

Because *she* is not the same.

She doesn't get your subtle hints or your mystery. She doesn't get your sense of humor or your sarcasm. She doesn't push you to talk about what's really bothering you and she doesn't know how to *comfort* you. She doesn't know how to make you smile and she doesn't know how to love you. You miss me because you finally realized how much I loved you and it's hitting you now that maybe *no one* will ever love you the way I did.

24

I Don't Smile Anymore When I Hear Your Name

I don't smile anymore when I hear your name. I don't feel the tingling sensation of our love returning to my body. In fact, I feel them *leaving*. Every time someone says your name I lose a little bit more love for you.

Your name doesn't remind me of long walks on the beach and conversations under the moonlight. It reminds me of cold nights and awkward silence. It reminds me of intimate details and secrets gone to waste.

Your name doesn't make me want to pick up the phone and call you like I used to. It reminds me of the nights I stayed next to my phone waiting for your name to pop up. It reminds of the final text you sent and how I turned my phone off and shoved it away.

Your name doesn't hold the same meaning like it used to. It doesn't reflect the greatest love of my life or my sweetest devotion. It means something else now – *indifference*. It means all my emotions detaching themselves from you and finding their way back to me. It means saving those emotions for someone who takes good care of them.

Your name doesn't sing the same song to my heart. It doesn't sing happy songs and beautiful words declaring love. I don't replay it in my head and I don't try to memorize it. I can barely hear it – the words are flat. For the first time I don't feel like singing along or even listening to it.

Your name doesn't make me empathetic either. I don't reminisce about what we had and try to bring it back, I don't see it as love lost anymore and I don't see it as *irreplaceable*. Your name makes me think of you as an experience, a memory, a lesson – a painting that was supposed to be beautiful but turned out all *squiggly*.

Your name doesn't remind me of warm fuzzy nights and clinking wine glasses. Every time someone mentions your name, the room gets colder. Every time someone mentions your name, I hear the wine glasses break piece by piece.

Your name doesn't make me want to look back anymore. I don't think of you and miss you. I don't wonder about you. Your name now makes me want to move on, it makes me want to walk away, and it makes me want to go to another place – a place where nobody says your name.

25

I'm Sorry I'm Not Fragile

I'm sorry I'm not fragile. I'm sorry if I move on when I have to because that means you can't ask for a second chance. I'm sorry if I don't look back and weep at the memories that we had together and dream of living them again. I'm sorry I don't have the urge to text you or call you when something reminds me of you.

I'm sorry I'm not fragile. I don't dwell on what could have been and why good things come to an end. I don't pray for you to come back and I don't ask everyone about you. I don't sleep in all day and drink all night to forget you. I'm sorry I'm not afraid of being alone.

I'm sorry I'm not scared of meeting someone new or falling in love again. I'm sorry your love didn't scar me. I'm not afraid of letting people in; you didn't make me want to build a wall or even a fence. I'm sorry I'm not fragile because I will love someone again with their darkness, I will not expect love to be easy or smooth – I will still give my heart out to those who are less than perfect and I will not expect them to rescue me from anything or rescue me from your love.

I'm sorry I am not empty. I have a life that fills me with joy,

I have friends that take up my whole life, and I have a family I can lean on. I have dreams I plan on achieving and I have places I plan on visiting – *with or without you.* I'm sorry you're not all I had, I'm sorry if you thought that my life revolved around you.

I'm sorry I'm not fragile. I don't break easily and the extra weight doesn't drag me down. I learned how to mend my heart and mend myself because everyday life invites me to dance and it would be a crime to stand still. I have seen too many broken souls who missed out on the beauty of life because they forgot to open up the blinds and I decided I will always let the light in.

I'm sorry if my strength makes me happy. *I'm sorry you think I am heartless for picking up the pieces that you broke and polishing them to shine brighter.* I'm sorry for smiling again like nothing ever took it away from me, I'm sorry you feel that you meant nothing to me. You meant a lot to me, but I mean *more* to me. But I want you to know that I *can* be fragile with a delicate heart and a soft soul, but with you I won't be.

I'm sorry I'm not fragile. I'm sorry you weren't able to change me, I'm sorry you had to watch someone fall out of love with you. I'm sorry that now you're going to have to look inside yourself and face your demons, I'm sorry that now you might have to hit rock bottom for a while and push everyone away from you. But I promise you that you will be fine, I promise that after the storm has passed, you will come out of it stronger and you won't be *fragile* anymore.

26

10 Reasons Why We Were Never Meant To Be

1. It took you so long to 'figure it out.'

You didn't feel that it was right in the depths of your heart, your mind didn't connect the dots that leads you back to my heart and you were *indifferent*. You can't be indifferent in love.

2. I was always trying too hard.

So you can see me, so you can love me, so you can appreciate me. I realize now that these are things you should've just seen naturally. I understand now that you can't make someone see your worth if they choose to keep looking the other way.

3. I was holding onto 'someday.'

A magical day when you finally realize how amazing this could be and how we really belong together. A day that kept me going when I had nothing else to believe in – a day I am now glad never happened.

4. You didn't really know who I was.

You didn't know my downfalls, you didn't know what makes me smile, you didn't know why some things scare me, and you didn't know what makes me feel *safe*.

5. We didn't share the same views on 'family'.

We didn't really have the same vision of what a home should feel like, we didn't share the same warmth and we didn't share the same *vows*.

6. Your friends saw more potential than you ever did.

They were rooting for us, for our story to come to fruition, they were rooting for an epic love story of two broken people who found a way to fix each other. **They didn't realize that two broken people can sometimes shatter each other to pieces.**

7. You introduced me to darkness.

Your love was like a tunnel, the further I got into it, the darker it got. I thought this was how love looks like from the inside, but I knew that this was a lie I created so I could stay. I wanted to escape to a love that offers an entire galaxy of shining lights.

8. I didn't listen.

To my friends, to my family, to your warning signs – to *you*. It's my fault for digging my own grave and expecting you to get me out of it. It's my fault that I counted on you to pick me up when you were kicking me when I was down.

9. Our words got lost in translation.

You never knew how to interpret my messages and I wasn't able to decode your encryption. We were reading the same book in two different languages and we couldn't find a translator for each other.

10. The distance kept growing.

The miles got longer and the nights got colder, we slowly drove away in different directions; you back to the *desert* and me back to the *land*. Our maps were never aligned. I could feel the poison leaving my body on the way back and realized our paths were meant to cross for a reason – so we can find our happiness somewhere else….away from each other.

27

Go Ahead And Leave

Go ahead and leave.

Leave the connection that you only come across once in your life. Leave the conversations that can go on forever and never lose their spark or their meaning. Leave the language of the eyes that penetrates through your soul. Leave the bond that seemed so real and effortless – leave the bond that somehow felt like magic.

Go ahead and run away.

Run away from your feelings, from the beauty of what could be. From the likelihood of finding the one love you've been looking for. Run away from the butterflies that keep hovering inside your whole body. Run away from the touch that softened your heart again, from the smile that made you forget your pain, from the eyes that got you lost in another world. Run away from something insanely fascinating. Run away from wonder.

Go ahead and hide.

Hide behind your work, your friends and your superficially predictable life. Hide behind your plans and your books and your goals. Hide from change, from the unknown, from the unfamiliar. Hide from something that could make you stop hiding once and for all. Hide from something that could change your life. Hide from something that only finds a special few people and it found you. Hide from something so rare; something that chose *you* out of billions of people.

Go ahead and escape.

Escape whatever moves you. Escape what makes you vulnerable or what makes you come alive. Escape what was once something you dreamed of finding. Escape the remedy to your virus, escape the angel to your demons, and the antidote to your poison.

Go ahead and walk away.

Walk far away from what you truly want. Stay trapped in your loneliness and your independence. Walk away from intimacy and affection. Walk away from hands that hold you at your worst and arms that hug you when you're tired. Walk away from ears that will listen to your doubts and your fears and eyes that will always see the best in you. Walk away from lips that will whisper so softly to you *'keep going'* that you will start to *believe* again.

Go ahead and disappear.

Disappear into the bubble you created – the one that keeps spinning around in the same place. The one that keeps turning your world upside down that you got used to living in an inverted reality. Slowly fade away till you're invisible. Fade away so no one sees who you really are. Fade away so no one knows how much you love them. Fade away till you are no longer whole again. Disappear and lose yourself.

Go ahead and get lost. Get so lost and run away from giving someone a chance to really find you.

28

The Truth About The Closure You Didn't Get

We don't really fall for someone thinking about how things will end – but we always hope that the ending will be clear and painless.

The recent trend is that people end things without closure; they could completely ghost you and abandon you or they could come up with some lame excuse explaining their sudden change in behavior. No matter what it is, it always feels like unfinished business and you long for just this one moment, this one conversation, this one heart to heart so you can understand what went wrong and get your closure. In my mind, most closures go something like this.

I'm sorry I wasn't strong enough to face you and tell you why I don't want to talk to you anymore. I realized that my feelings have changed along the way and I didn't want to hurt you by telling you that I am not the person you thought I was.

I'm sorry I checked out without warning, I knew you were getting attached and I just had to cut the strings before you hold on to them too tightly. **I wasn't ready to be the one to pull you through.**

I'm sorry you had to deal with all the confusion, self-doubt and unanswered questions. The answer was simple; I had other things on my mind, we were not on the same page and I didn't want to be the one you run to when you needed someone. I wanted you to feel how unreliable I was so you wouldn't rely on me.

I apologize for painting a happy picture only to tear it down later, I was living in the moment and I didn't consider your feelings. Part of me thought this might work and the other didn't want to even try. I am sorry I was in limbo and you were caught in the middle of it all.

I'm sorry you thought I was better than that, you deserve better than that, you deserved an explanation, you deserve a good reason for my sudden departure and I'm sorry you didn't get it. I'm sorry if that will build your walls up higher for the next person, I'm sorry you now think everyone will leave without warning. **I'm sorry your heart is now broken to love deeply again.**

————

The truth about the closure you didn't get is that it was a *choice*. Someone chose to ignore your questions, disregard your feelings and insult your intelligence. Someone chose not to send that text or give you the final call or look at you and tell you why they need to leave.

The truth about the closure you didn't get is that you actually got it. No closure is somehow closure. No closure means that someone didn't care enough about you to talk to you like you matter, they didn't care about how you will see them, they didn't care about how your friends will see them, they didn't care about how they will face you again when you run into them and they didn't care about how fragile your heart was. They decided to be selfish and greedy. They decided to take without giving back.

So this is the closure you really need: how someone else closed their door doesn't define how you should close *yours*. Just because someone left doesn't mean that everyone will leave. No matter how many doors people close, you have to always leave yours open because someone will come knocking on your door and will never want to leave.

Part 3

When Friends Become Family & Family Becomes Friends

29

10 Things You Learn From Being Raised By A Strong Mother

1. You learn the value of independence.

You don't need a man to save you or anyone to take care of you, you learn by example that you are capable of living a full and happy life without having to share it with someone else. You learn that you can build a home, raise kids, cook, and do the dishes all while having a thriving career. You pretty much learn how to be super woman.

2. You learn the meaning of unconditional love.

You saw your mom sacrifice her time, health and youth for you and your siblings, yet she never complained or gloated about how much she is suffering or how much she is doing. She always had a smile on her face and was happily giving more and more of herself. She taught you what selfless and unconditional love looks like, and you know you won't be able to find that love anywhere else.

3. You learn how to love yourself.

You learn how to walk away from the things that are not meant for you, you learn how to keep going even when the whole world is against you, and you learn how to believe in yourself when everyone is doubting you. You learn that bad grades, heart breaks and failures don't define you; what defines you is how you bounce back from all the setbacks and how hard you fight for the life you want.

4. You learn that you can be both strong and soft.

Strong mothers are usually very sensitive they just hide it better, but you saw your mom silently cry over your pain, or stay up all night taking care of you when you were sick, or the nights she couldn't sleep because something was troubling you. The way she hugs you when you are down shows unmatched compassion and tenderness and sometimes in a quiet corner you saw her shed a few tears.

5. You learn that it's not easy being a woman.

You learn that your opinion will be discounted, that you will be taken lightly when you're being serious, but you will also learn that you can stand out in a crowd and force everyone to listen to your voice and accept your ideas. You learn that what doesn't kill you makes you stronger.

6. You learn never to look back.

You learn to let all the "what ifs" and "could have beens" go. You learn not to look back and wonder why life turned upside down. You just keep looking forward and let the past redeem itself. You learn that everything that happened got you to where you belong even if it is nothing you ever wished for.

7. You learn the importance of patience and faith.

You learn that God is looking out for you and your struggles, that everything will be OK in the end. Storms will pass and tomorrow is a new day. You learn to be patient with life, patient with timing, patient with success and patient with problems. You learn that *patience is strength*.

8. You learn how to create your own happiness.

You can find happiness in a difficult life. You can still be happy even if you are carrying the weight of the world on your shoulders. My mom taught me that I can always find something to smile about all I have to do is look closer.

9. You learn that she still knows more about love than you do.

Even when you are generations apart, even if you are not fond of her love choices, if she doesn't approve of someone you better listen to her. She knows what she is saying; moreover, she doesn't want to see you get heartbroken. As much as I hate to admit it, she got it right every time.

10. You learn how to be a good mother.

You've been raised by a mom who showed you how to truly take care of a family, who showed you that hard work pays off, who showed you that you can love someone unconditionally. She showed you how to be protective, loving, kind, compassionate, strong and resilient. She was leading by example, and whether you know it or not, you are following in her footsteps one step at a time.

30

40 Signs Your Best Friends Are Basically Your Family

1. You always call them first, when you have good news or bad news.

2. You rely on them for advice on everything from what to wear to whether or not you should break up with someone you're dating.

3. You find excuses to celebrate life together in addition to all the regular champagne worthy occasions (birthdays, anniversaries, big presentations…etc.)

4. You understand them better than you understand most (if not all) of your family members.

5. You know everything there is to know about their daily lives, their innermost desires and their biggest problems.

6. You confess things to them long before you share things with your family.

7. You stalk them on social media because you're their diehard super fan.

8. You can trust them not to tag you in any unflattering pictures.

9. You get jealous when they form new friendships.

10. You know you're completely immune from judgment in their eyes.

11. You buy them gifts and cute souvenirs whenever you see something they might like.

12. You lean on them (literally, on the couch when you're chilling together) and figuratively more than you ever lean on your bio family.

13. You are the happiest you when you're with them.

14. You can be silly & goofy or moody & grumpy and they'll tolerate you anyway.

15. You want them to know everything, even the unnecessary details.

16. You miss them like crazy when they're away.

17. You get separation anxiety when it's been too long since you last saw them.

18. You appreciate them—truly, madly, deeply.

19. You call them to just to say "I love you."

20. You rarely fight, and when you do, resolution comes quickly.

21. You never have to explain or defend yourself to them.

22. You know in your heart that they'll never let you down.

23. You know you can trust them with your most intimate secrets.

24. You don't have to keep up appearances in their company.

25. You don't have to pretend that you like the food they cook for you.

26. You only want to travel with them.

27. You've known each other forever, it seems, even during past lives.

28. You know their past and you have been through it all together.

29. You believe them when they tell you who you really are.

30. You consult them when you need a pep talk.

31. You laugh the hardest when you are with them.

32. You cry the hardest when you are with them.

33. You always manage to make time for them, even when you're busy.

34. You never need your space from them.

35. You see yourself perfectly capable of living with them without going crazy.

36. You kind of resemble them.

37. You never have to worry that they'll take something you say the wrong way.

38. You know all their passwords and they know yours.

39. You *chose* them.

40. You can't live without them.

<u>31</u>

20 Ways An Older Brother Prepares You For The Big Bad World

1. He toughens you up at a young age.

Older brother might as well be another word for *tough love*. From giving you a hard time about literally everything in your life, to being a little bit mean/brutally honest to you at times, older brothers have a way of subconsciously building strength and power within you.

2. He brings the inner competitor in you.

Whether you are yearning to prove him wrong, or even show your parents that you can be cool too. You will find yourself drawing inspiration from him, he will challenge you to get out of your comfort zone.

3. He is the cool dad you always wished for.

There are some things you can't tell your dad that you will definitely tell your brother. He will be more open minded and more understanding when you talk to him about issues that your dad will never comprehend.

4. He is your lawyer.

He will cover up for you when you mess up and take the blame from time to time. One thing about older brothers, they have a way with parents and always know how to get their sisters out of trouble.

5. He doesn't let you get away with things.

If you think you evaded your parents with his help. He will be there to pick up the pieces and then throw them back at you!

6. He has a BS radar.

If he doesn't approve of the new friend you made in school, or the man you like, listen to him. He has a radar for who is not genuine with his sister or who is about to screw his sister over.

7. He is always right.

You may not always listen to him, but as much as you hate to admit it, he knows what he is talking about, and unfortunately is *always right*.

8. His words may hurt you.

Older brothers are not sensitive with their words, and won't frost their words to make you feel better. They will hit you with the truth like a bat and it will hurt, but it will open to your eyes to the *truth* your were too blind to see.

9. He is secretly your best-friend.

He was your best friend before you even had friends, he was there when you had no one and he always had your back.

10. He gives you the keys to understand men.

Just by living with him or eavesdropping on his conversations with his friends. You know a great deal about men and how they think, you probably know *too much*.

11. He knows how to make you laugh.

And forget about your sorrows. He knows all your embarrassing memories, he has seen you make a fool of yourself. It is always refreshing to talk to him when you are down.

12. He introduces you to new sports, video games, and cooler music.

You were always ahead of the curve because your brother passed his progressive tastes and gadgets on to you.

13. He is your tutor.

He helped you study when you were struggling with a subject, but more importantly, he helped you study people, he helped you study life, he helped you study *adulthood*.

14. He sets the bar pretty high.

You know a certain kind of love and protection that you can't fall short of. This is why you have high standards, it is hard to find someone who can measure up to him, even harder to find someone that he approves of.

15. He is your personal FBI.

He will be the first to investigate this new friend or love interest and come up with a full report better than any extensive FBI report. Never underestimate the ability of an older brother to find things out.

16. People suck up to you.

Girls will talk you because you have a handsome older brother, boys will talk to you because they want to hang out with your cool older brother. Either way–you win.

17. Wherever you go, you will be taken good care of.

Because people know your brother and respect him, they will always be extra nice to you. For some reason, people respect you more when they know you have an older brother–society works in mysterious ways.

18. He is your technician, your mover, your IT consultant and your handy man.

Pretty much he is there to fix anything that needs fixing–including *you*.

19. He is your call to the rescue.

Flat tire? Creepy man following you? You're having a nervous breakdown? Can't open your new peanut butter jar? Your older brother will always be your call to the rescue, no matter how much you fight or argue, when all hell breaks loose, you won't call anyone but him; not your dad, not your boyfriend or husband, not your best friend- you, will call your brother, because you know that no matter what, he will be your savior.

20. He is your safe haven.

There is a sense of safety and security in knowing you have an older brother you can depend on and rely on in times of need. In a way, he is your superhero.

32

15 Reasons Why Your 'Cool Aunt' Is The Ultimate Best Friend

1. She was your partner in crime growing up.

She let you get away with things you would've gotten in trouble for. She told you family secrets you weren't supposed to know, and she would always sneak you candy or anything you were not supposed to have.

2. She is the one you go to for guy advice.

Because she won't freak out like your mom and won't let you do whatever you want like your friends. She is the perfect person to talk to about the guy you're unsure of or the guy you just started talking to or the guy you want to bring home.

3. She is the one you love to drink with.

She was probably the one who gave you your first drink or the one who thinks there's nothing a drink couldn't fix.

4. She is the one you call when you're helpless.

Not only will she tell you what to do, she might drop whatever she is doing and come help you. Cool aunts are usually tougher than most people and will not let their nieces go astray.

5. She stands up for you in front of your parents.

She knows you and she always sees your point of view and speaks on your behalf when your parents are against you.

6. She is the one you look up to.

You admire her strength, her charisma, her flexibility and her resilience; how she can act like a mother one day and a 10-year-old kid the next. You admire how she lives life to the fullest no matter what life hands her.

7. She helped you understand your parents.

She knows them and she knows you and she is always telling you stories about their past so you can understand them better. She is the one who helped you love them when they were being hard to love.

8. She encouraged your rebellious phase.

Even though she was worried, she encouraged you to go out and explore the world the way you saw it. She wanted you to become your own person like she did. Even when your parents almost gave up on you, she knew you will always find your way. She sees herself in you and she gets it.

9. She knows all your friends.

She may even join your ladies night from time to time. They all love her and ask about her. She is always cracking jokes and making fun of them and of course she is just as generous with them as she is with you.

10. She is the one you confide in.

She knows your darkest secrets, the ones you can't tell your friends about and the ones you surely can't tell your mom about. You know they are safe with her and you know she will never hold them against you.

11. She has the last word.

Even though you act like you listen to your mom or you need her approval, it's really your aunt that has the last word. You trust her opinion more, you trust her judgment and you trust her blindly because she knows you better than you know yourself.

12. She knows how to make you smile.

You've probably spent plenty of nights at her house because

you just couldn't deal with anyone. She is the only one you can take in full doses and she always knows how to comfort you. She is always the one you go to when you feel like no one understands you.

13. She still spoils you.

No matter how old you are, you will always be her baby niece, and she will forever pamper you like you were first-born. Birthdays or not; she never comes empty-handed.

14. She is your person.

She is your first and real best friend, because she knew you when you were a baby and she knew your parents when they were young and reckless and she knew the family secrets so you don't have to explain anything to her. She knows it all and she knows how to solve your problems. Your conversations can go on forever and it will only feel like a minute.

15. She loves you unconditionally.

Whether she has kids or not, whether she is close to your mom or not, whether you are the golden girl or a hot mess, she just loves you wholeheartedly. She chose you, she was the one who decided she wants to be your best friend rather than your aunt. You will have a special place in her heart and she is not afraid to tell the whole world that you are her favorite niece.

33

25 Things You Forgot To Thank Your Soul Sister For

1. For understanding you when you couldn't understand yourself.

2. For being patient enough to listen to you babble on about everything and nothing with a smile on her face.

3. For forgiving you when you were too self-absorbed to ask about her.

4. For understanding your unusual love choices because she probably has the same taste.

5. For being selfless and inspiring you to be a better person.

6. For being just as crazy as you are and encouraging you to embrace your inner weirdo.

7. For being the best wing woman and telling you when and how many times your crush has looked at you.

8. For getting your lame jokes and loving them.

9. For replaying your silliest and goofiest snapchats and sending goofier ones back.

10. For letting you borrow her favorite dress for whatever occasion you had and didn't mind you spilling wine all over it.

11. For helping you write and re-write the text message you've been wanting to send and taking out all those emojis.

12. For knowing when something is wrong with you even when you try to hide it, and then doing what she has to do to make it better.

13. For going out of her way to make you happy even if she had a bad day.

14. For always pointing out the good things in you and pushing you to love yourself.

15. For all the happy memories she brought into your life and for giving you so many amazing experiences to look back on.

16. For loving your weird family just as they are.

17. For supporting your plans whether you stick to them or not.

18. For remembering important job events and sending you sweet messages about them.

19. For thinking about you and sending you pictures even when she is traveling.

20. For letting you have the last slice of pizza.

21. For holding you when you couldn't stop crying.

22. For signing up to all the odd yoga classes you've been wanting to try.

23. For talking you up in front of everyone; making you feel like a queen.

24. For always being honest with you, even if it's not what you want to hear.

25. For being in your life. Simply she just makes your life better in every possible way.

34

30 Things You Forgot To Thank Your Best Guy Friend For

1. For listening to your "girly" stories and trying to understand them.

2. For accepting your love-crazy phase, your dramatic phase, your rebellious phase or any other random phase you went through.

3. For being your call to the rescue when you are in trouble.

4. For being your call to the rescue when you are heartbroken.

5. For giving you the best guy advice and making you realize how clueless you really are.

6. For keeping your secrets–the ones you can never tell your girl friends.

7. For forgiving you when you drifted apart because the guy you dated didn't like how close you two were.

8. For hanging out with you at the most random times in the most random places.

9. For helping you send that text without looking like a fool.

10. For letting you interrupt him while he is watching an important game to tell him something.

11. For being the best & funniest wing-man.

12. For standing up for you when someone hurts you.

13. For picking you up when you didn't have a ride.

14. For being your plus one to the awkward family wedding you didn't want to go to alone.

15. For tolerating your obsession with Gossip Girl & One Tree Hill without judging you.

16. For telling the girl he dates that you are his *real* best friend.

17. For liking all your selfies.

18. For introducing you to the new (somewhat disgusting) slang and things guys talk about.

19. For blocking all the douchebags from talking to you when you are out having fun.

20. For being the brother you always wished for.

21. For staying in touch when you moved away.

22. For being your biggest fan and supporting all your bizarre endeavors.

23. For telling you he won't date a girl unless you approve of her.

24. For caring about your problems and asking you about them until they are no longer bothering you.

25. For helping you get over your heartbreak by making you laugh hysterically.

26. For letting you crash guys night when you had no one else to go out with.

27. For letting you see his softer and more romantic side when he is in love.

28. For telling you the truth no matter how hard it is

29. For reassuring you that you will always be his best friend even if you don't see or talk to each other as much as you used to.

30. For being the only man in your life who will never walk away.

35

10 Reasons Why Your College Friends Will Always Have A Special Place In Your Heart

1. They've seen you at your absolute worst.

When you were stressed out before your finals, or working day and night on your thesis. They've seen your mood swings, your rants and your melt downs and they totally understood where it was coming from.

2. They witnessed your dating nightmares.

All of them – on or off campus. College is the hub of all dating mistakes and lessons and your college friends have seen all the stages of dating you went through one after the other.

3. They were there for you.

They helped you make it through the tough times, they would take notes for you if you were sick, and they would have a slumber party just for you if you were down. They were there for the highs and the lows and they were always there when you truly needed them.

4. They've learned not to judge you.

They understood your quirks and accepted it. Too bossy in group projects? Too lazy to even participate? You joke too much while studying? They've learned to accept you for who you are and love you for it.

5. They've shared countless memories with you.

They were part of every crazy college story you had and you have stories together for life. They know too much and they've seen too much. Your college friends will always be your ultimate partners in crime.

6. Meeting up with them is always delightful.

Your time with them is still the best. Stories get funnier as you get older and you still remember all the details like it was yesterday. You remind each other of the things you used to do, the people you used to date and how the hell you guys made it through finals. It's always full of both laughter and embarrassment.

7. They understand you better than anyone.

They were the closest ones to you when you were *really* growing up and trying to be an adult. You were all finding your-selves together. You shared the same phase and you went through the same changes. So you understand each other's struggles and know how to comfort each other.

8. They are your biggest fans.

They know your real dreams – you've talked about it together and talked about where you all want to be in ten years, so when you finally achieve what you've been dreaming of, they cheer you on like they did in your thesis presentation. They know how hard you worked for it and how badly you wanted it.

9. They are the reason behind the best days of your life.

They will always be the main reason why you enjoyed college and why you miss it. You miss seeing them every day and talk-ing to them for hours, you miss making fun of each other, you miss trying to give each other horrible advice and you miss how they always managed to make you laugh no matter how stressed you were.

10. They will always be in your life because you *chose* them.

You weren't forced to sit next to them in class, you weren't forced to work with them on projects, and you weren't forced to travel with them. You chose them – every step of the way. No matter how many friends you make, your college friends will always hold a special place in your heart.

36

10 Different Types Of Friends Every Girl Needs In Her Life

1. The childhood bestie.

She's your person, your best friend and your sister. She knows too much about you ever since you were 10. She is the one who has been through thick and thin with you and will always be in your life. She is your soul sister.

2. The crazy one.

The one who is up for anything. She is the one who pushes you to do unusual things and break the rules. She is the one you call when you are indecisive about making a bad decision because you know she will encourage you to go ahead and do it. She is the one you always have fun with no matter what's going on in your life.

3. The mother.

She is the one who takes care of you and all her other friends. She makes sure she has everything you can think of in her purse; in case of emergency. She always has an extra charger, a Band-Aid, Airborne, and anything you might need. She is your parent's favorite because she keeps you out of trouble.

4. The brutally honest one.

She is the one who tells it like it is–no *sugar coating* whatsoever. She is the one who will tell you the guy you like is a douche, or you are a douche or whatever comes to her mind. She is your reality check.

5. The dating expert.

AKA Samantha from SATC. She's dated the entire universe and is the source of all your dating tips and tricks. She has dated all sorts of guys and knows how to spot a liar, a cheater, a player or a keeper. She is your ideal wing woman.

6. The hustler.

She is the one who knows how to make things happen. She is killing at work, at the gym, or at the groceries. She knows all the shortcuts, all the sales and all the events that are happening that no one knows about. She is the one who is always traveling and meeting prominent people. She is definitely the one you go to talk about your dreams because she will connect you with all the right people or get you an upgrade practically anywhere.

7. The funny one.

The one with all the jokes and the stories; she never runs out of stories that crack everyone up. She is also the sarcastic one who will make fun of your boyfriend, your clothes, your new friend, your car and anything that she feels like mocking. She is one you chill with even if you don't feel like being around people.

8. Your favorite coworker.

She is your work bestie. You go to lunch together, you are always chatting on the company's messenger, you bitch about your bosses together, and you have explored every single happy hour spot in the city. You know that she will be your friend for life even if you get a new job.

9. The long lost-twin.

The one you met recently but clicked with right away. You keep discovering how much you two have in common and your relationship is just a bunch of *high-fives* and *ME TOOs*. She is one you feel like you've known forever and you can easily understand each other really since you two are essentially the same person.

10. The dude.

Your boy. Your sidekick. Your wing man. He is your best guy friend who decided to accept and love you unconditionally.

He is your go to person when you are in trouble, when you want to have a good time, when you need guy advice or when you simply can't keep with all the 'girls' drama. He plays a very important role in your life.

37

To The Boy Who Let My Best Friend Go

I'd love to see you in a few years when you are standing there watching how happy she is with someone else and you get that hint of sadness and regret in your heart that you let someone amazing go. You let go of someone who was ready to give you her world. You let go of someone who would've never let go of you.

As I listened to her cry over you, I couldn't help but wonder what kind of person you really are. What kind of man do you really want to be? Do you find joy in leading women on? Do you find joy in making women fall in love with you then run away before you can catch them?

Regardless of what kind of man you are, let me tell you what kind of woman you let go of.

You let go of a woman who knew from the day she met you that she wanted to do nothing but love you, and love you with all her heart. Someone who told the whole world that she is in love with a wonderful man. Someone who told the world that she will not even look at any other man because all she sees is you. Someone who was ready to give up her world for you.

You let go of a woman who saw greatness in you even when

you couldn't see it in yourself. Someone who believed in you more than she believed in herself. Someone who was willing to stand by you through thick and thin and patiently wait for you as you figure out your life, your career and *yourself.*

You let go of a woman who once said to me that you are all she ever wished for, she once believed you are the answer to all her prayers. *You let go of someone who believed that you were her destiny, you let go of someone who had unwavering faith in you.* I wonder if you saw how happy she was with you and how the smile never left her face. I wonder if you have any heart at all to willingly take that smile away.

You let go of a woman who fought for you. She fought with her friends when they doubted you, she fought with her parents when they asked if you were serious about her, and she fought her own thoughts when they warned her about you. She fought for you over and over again. I wonder if you knew how hard she fought for you and how every time she would fight for you; she would lose some of her *own strength.* I wonder if you ever ask yourself if you were even worth that fight.

I say 'boy' because this is exactly what you are. You're a boy who took the love of an amazing girl for granted, you were selfish, immature and insecure and she made you love yourself. You loved how she made you feel, you kept giving her small doses of love to keep her going until you felt good about yourself again and no longer needed her attention.

You're a boy for not being honest about your intentions and your future plans. You're a boy for making someone tear down their walls only to build your own walls higher. You're a boy for making someone open up to you only to close yourself off. You're a boy for promising love to someone only to break their heart.

I would like to tell you that I'm not worried about her, she will be fine a lot sooner than you think. She's got friends who will stand by her and make her forget you even existed. That's how much she is *loved* and that's how much you should've loved her. It's you who I'm worried about; I'm worried about the kind of man you're becoming, I'm worried about the women that you will keep dragging along on your roller coaster. I'm worried about the friends you will start losing as you continue down that selfish path. *I'm worried about the hearts that you will keep on breaking in an attempt to fix yours.*

I'm worried about you but not because I care about you – not at all. I'm worried about you because amazing women like my best friend believe in boys like you and they end up getting heartbroken. I'm worried about the number of best friends who will want to write you the same letter one day. I hope you realize that women are not *toys*. I hope you realize that if you don't know how to give love then you should stop looking for it. I know one day you will regret letting her go, and if you don't, I hope you realize that you only paved the way for some-one much better to come into her life. You taught her how to look for a man – not another boy.

38

To My Best Friend On Her Wedding Day: 30 Things I Want You Know

1. Today is the first day of your new life with him. And he is lucky because you will make his mornings brighter and his nights sweeter.

2. I know he is your man now but you can still count on me.

3. The day we've been dreaming about is finally here and I know you are smiling because you finally realized I was right when I told you he will find you one day.

4. I know you're looking back and laughing at all the frogs you've kissed before and how hung up you were on them and I know you're smiling because these days are over and you found a real man who can cherish you and appreciate you.

5. I will cry during my toast – I apologize in advance for ruining your makeup.

6. If you ever feel like you're not good enough for him, I want you to remember today and the way he looked at you as you were walking down the aisle.

7. Ever since I met him and I knew he deserved you, I'm sorry I gave him a hard time but I had to make sure that he is willing to fight for you.

8. I hope he loves you in a way that makes you believe in love every single day and tell your mom how happy he makes you so she can finally sleep at night.

9. I hope he listens to you when you're down and go out of his way to make you smile.

10. I hope he likes your weird obsessions and your eccentric tastes, I hope he supports your dreams even if he can't understand them.

11. I hope he always puts you first, I hope he knows that life is incomplete without you, that all the good things in life won't mean a thing if he is not sharing them with you. I hope you become the only thing he truly can't live without.

12. I hope he understands that I am not going anywhere and he should expect me to show up uninvited and call you whenever I feel like it.

13. I hope you can completely be yourself with him; with all your flaws and imperfections, I hope he finds them endearing and beautiful and doesn't try to change them.

14. Even though I hate to give up my spot, but I hope he becomes your best friend, the one you can talk to about anything, the one you can trust with your life, the one you can reveal your secrets to and know that he won't judge you. I hope he becomes the male version of me.

15. I hope you can sit together in silence and still be happy, I hope you can have endless conversations with him and not get bored.

16. I hope you're finally happy that you will be able to have someone for the holidays, someone you can spoil and cook for. Someone to just cuddle with in front of the Christmas tree and sing 'All I Want For Christmas' to.

17. If he ever hurts you, I hope he knows you have an army of women ready to take him down.

18. If he ever hurts you, I hope you know that you can always come crying to me no matter how long we've gone without talking to each other.

19. I hope he fulfills all his vows and I hope he promises more as time goes by.

20. He will give you the kids you always wanted and you will love him even more for it.

21. I hope your daughter has your sense of humor and your kindness. And I hope your son has his chivalry and his determination.

22. I will come to your daughter's dance recitals and your son's football games. Save a spot for me.

23. We'll still have our inside jokes that he will never get.

24. Even though I will still see you, I will miss the random adventures and random trips we used to take. I will miss the days when you had all the time in the world for me, now I have to share it with someone else.

25. I will always be the one you fell in love with at first sight.

26. I promise you I will be his friend too and try to understand him, but he has to know that I will always be on your side.

27. I want you to know that you are a person worthy of all the love in the world and that you make him happy – even if you don't believe it, you do! You make people happy.

28. I want you to know that you give me hope, and you always did. You gave me hope that love exists and that it can be both pure and strong and it can definitely heal people. Your love is mystical.

29. I want you to know that as you walk away with him to start a new life that it will not always be easy, but if you can love him and forgive him as much as you love me and forgive me – your marriage will last and it will blossom and it will only grow stronger.

30. I want you to know that no matter what, I'll always be there for you and I will never stop loving you.

Part 4

The Journey To Becoming Who You Really Are

Maybe the journey isn't so much about becoming anything. Maybe it's about unbecoming everything that isn't you so you can be who you were meant to be in the first place.
— *Unknown*

39

15 Things You No Longer Have To Apologize For

1. Don't apologize for being real in a world where being real only gets you so far.

2. Don't apologize for cutting toxic people out of your life no matter how long you have known them, how close you were or even if you are related.

3. Don't apologize for ignoring their text message after going months without hearing from them.

4. Don't apologize for posting that quote or song or article that may offend some people, post them and tell those people to get over themselves.

5. Don't apologize for being a little bit more guarded.

6. Don't apologize for deciding not to love someone who did you wrong.

7. Don't apologize for neglecting people who only need you when it's convenient for them.

8. Don't apologize for the painful things you said, because if they can say it, why can't you?

9. Don't apologize for trusting all the wrong people, because they taught you that some people may seem to want all the best for you, but when you get it, they want to take it away.

10. Don't apologize for celebrating even if there is nothing to celebrate, because fun should not be tied to certain occasions, people, achievements or materials.

11. Don't apologize for not keeping things to yourself anymore — get it off your chest so you can breathe again.

12. Don't apologize for calling someone out, it is your right to set boundaries in every relationship.

13. Don't apologize for putting yourself first, because let's face it — someone had to.

14. Don't apologize for being an adult who is still learning what matters, who matters, and which direction to go.

15. Don't apologize for simply becoming who you are meant to be.

40

10 Struggles Only People Who Are Hard On Themselves Will Understand

1. You can't fall asleep peacefully.

Bed time is the worst for you because you replay every single interaction in your head and how it could've been better or what you should have said instead. And sometimes you remember things you've done years ago and beat yourself up for it.

2. You are never satisfied.

No matter how talented you are or how much praise you're getting, you will always feel like you could do better or your work isn't good enough. The smallest error could mean the end of the world to you.

3. You don't like asking for help even when you need it.

Because it makes you feel weak and incapable of helping yourself. And when you ask for it, you feel like you are committing a crime. You want to do everything by yourself and you don't want to cause anyone any inconvenience.

4. You feel bad if your friends are not having a good time.

You feel responsible for their happiness. You see it as your problem that they aren't having a good time and you try to solve it.

5. You can't stop thinking about any minor criticism you've received.

You are already self-critical, so when someone reaffirms your flaws or errors, you can remember it for months and months to come and won't be happy until you fix it.

6. Yet you never believe compliments.

If someone compliments you, you automatically think they're just being nice to you or they don't mean what they say. And of course you rarely give yourself any compliments.

7. You hate exposing your vulnerability.

You don't want people to know that you may not be as strong as you seem. You are known to be tough and you don't want anything to change that. You even hate being vulnerable with your closest friends or family.

8. You think people will never forgive you.

If you make a small mistake or if you offended someone, you always believe that this person will never forgive you for it and will remember it every time they see you. You fear that things will never be the same again. *You expect people to be hard on you too.*

9. You apologize a lot.

For the things you did and the things you didn't do. You sometimes apologize for traffic, storms or anything that you have no control over. Saying sorry comes naturally to you.

10. You don't know how to receive love.

You think that you have so many things to work on and improve that it's so hard for anyone to love you. Even when someone does, you think it's temporary, not real or not genuine. You expect people to walk away from you once they get to know who you really are. This is why you are *emotionally guarded* and find it very hard to let people in. You are definitely your own worst enemy.

41

10 Meaningful Words Every 20-Something Ends Up Redefining

As I approach the final year of my twenties, I can't help but look back on my life and all the changes and growth my twenties brought. I feel like I am a different person than I was five years ago, actually, I feel like I am a different person than I was two years ago. My definition of everything has changed, my heart changed and my mind surely did change. The twenties are fun and exciting, but they are also confusing and painful. However, if lived right or *wrong* depending on how you look at it, they can offer valuable lessons, and mistakes you can avoid in your thirties. As you walk down that road, you will have to stop and redefine some things.

1. Happiness

Redefine happiness to revolve around achieving goals, life-long experiences, and genuine relationships. Look for more long-term and intrinsic happiness instead of short-term pleasures. Your happiness is defined by what inspires you and what keeps your soul and mind rested not by what keep you up at night.

2. Love

Love takes a new direction in your late twenties. You no longer try to find someone who is all about fun and games, you want someone to listen to the words you whisper, and understand the depth in your eyes. You want someone who will put out the fire burning within you and assures you that they want to be part of your book, not just a sentence in your chapter.

3. Beauty

The definition of beauty goes beyond looks. You find grace beautiful, you find maturity sexy, you find responsibility gorgeous and most importantly; you find honesty jaw-dropping. Even the way you define beauty for yourself changes. You are no longer focused on how you should look or what you should wear, you are working on beauty that has no expiration date.

4. Friendship

Friends become your second family, you are more interested in friendships that last and stand the test of time. You look for friends you can call at 5 am and friends you can confide in. You don't trust as much people as you used to and you don't respect as much people as you used to. Your friends are your sanctuary and you make sure to keep it safe.

5. Success

Success becomes a journey not a destination. It becomes in the balance and harmony of your life rather than how much money you make and what kind of car you drive. It is not the noise around you but the stillness within your heart. It is not in the quantity of things in your life but the quality of it.

6. Fun

You no longer feel the need to be everywhere, or attend every party you are invited to. Fun is defined by who you are with and how happy you are when you are with them. It doesn't matter if it's at home or at fancy restaurant. Fun is multiplied when it is simplified.

7. Attraction

You redefine what you want to attract and who you want to attract. You no longer try to attract what is popular or what is easy or what makes sense. You attract what you truly desire, you attract who you see a future with, you attract wander that doesn't leave you wondering if it was attractive.

8. Strength

You redefine strength by how far you've come, by the moments of weakness you overcame, by the smiles you fought through your tears. Your strength is in the fact that you are still standing on your own two feet.

9. Time

You lose your attachment to time as you go on. You are no longer forcing yourself to do something or find someone by a certain age. You cherish your time and you make sure you spend it by doing things that will make you grow and around people who make it fly. You make time for your priorities, and you make sure time doesn't pass you by.

10. Yourself

Probably the most important redefinition of all – YOU. As you grow older, you will realize that you will have to do a lot of things alone. You will have to be your own hero and you will have to pick yourself up sometimes. You will redefine what you care about, what you are chasing, what you are believing in, what you are looking forward to and what you want to achieve. You will redefine how you see yourself and how you want to be seen. You will redefine how you want to spend the rest of your life, and you will redefine whether or not you want your life to have meaning and if you want the world to understand it.

42

10 Pieces Of Advice I Wish I Had Listened To When I Was Younger

I don't regret much in my life because everything you go through is meant to teach you something. However, I regret not listening to the words of those who knew what they were talking about. The words that were so simple to understand yet so hard to follow.

1. Do what you love and success will follow.

After college, our focus becomes how to make money, that we often pick a career that we do not love. We forget that we are choosing a career that we are going to have to stick to for a very long time and a life spent doing that work. Ironically, you're *more likely* to make money if you love what you do because you will simply never get enough of it. Take the time to figure out what it is you love to do.

2. Don't worry about what others may think of you.

I spent so much time trying to please people and consider what they might say or think if I do something unconventional, until I realized that people are never pleased and they will find something to pick on or talk about. While it's important to be considerate of others, **don't let their thoughts limit yours.**

3. He/she is just not that into you.

Instead of wasting months and years trying to translate text messages, interpret mixed signals or closely look for signs of interest, your time is better off spent being with someone who doesn't make you question the simplest methods of communication or look for elusive signs.

4. You are the average of the five people you spend the most time with.

In other words; *choose your friends wisely.* They will play an important role in your life and will have a profound impact on your decisions. Choose your inner circle wisely and make sure they want the best for you.

5. Sleep on it.

This is precious. I've been known to destroy things because I am impulsive and impatient. The best piece of advice I received when I was hesitant, or angry or hurt is to sleep on whatever it is that was bothering me and make a decision the next morning. It's amazing what 6 hours of sleep can do to your mind and your decisions.

6. If you keep doing what you're doing, you'll keep getting what you're getting.

As simple as it sounds, if you want to change something in your life, you will have to do things differently or change something within yourself. Insanity is doing the same thing over and over again and expecting different results.

7. You can't learn to swim without getting in the water.

You can't experience life just by observing and you can't know how something works unless you try it. Taking risks and trying new things is the best way for us to get to know ourselves and understand our lives and truly *learn* from our own experiences.

8. Don't expect people to treat you the way you treat them.

If you expect someone to be good to you just because you are good to them, or someone to like you just because you like them, you are setting yourself up for disappointment. When it comes to people, it's best to drop all expectations and give without expecting anything in return. You only have control over *you*–not anyone else.

9. You have to learn how to be alone.

It took me a very long time to be OK with this. I used to think that being alone is the worst thing that can happen to anyone. But I realized that sometimes it's pivotal to be on your own to figure things out and grow as an individual. We can't guarantee that people will be there for us when we need them to, and one of the best lessons we can learn in life is how to be *comfortable* with being alone. It will empower us.

10. What's meant to be will be.

It may sound like a cliché but it's the ultimate truth. We can't control our fate because some things will always be unknown to us. Time solves everything, and we will get the answers we were desperately looking for when we are *ready* for them.

43

This Is How To Be Happy: 15 Things Truly Happy People Do Differently

1. They find healthy ways to cope with stress and anxiety.

Whether it's going for a walk, running, kick-boxing, writing, or simply meditating or listening to music. They find prolific outlets to cope with their sadness instead of drowning in a sea of self-sabotage and despair.

2. They are grateful for the things they have *now*.

They don't dwell on what they've lost or wait and wish for what they want. They simply enjoy what they have now and they know how to make it enough for them to be happy.

3. They don't take life too seriously.

They laugh easily and try not to take things too personally. They know how to find joy in the simplest moments of life.

4. They don't hold grudges.

They forgive and forget, they try to live without any ill feelings, because they understand that this will only harm them. They sincerely let go of people who did them wrong, and forgive them even if they are not sorry.

5. They say yes more than no.

They have an open mind about trying new things and talking to different people. They are interested in experiencing life with all its glory. They are passionately curious and easygoing.

6. They pick happy friends.

They hang out with positive and happy people. They know that happiness is multiplied when its divided and the happier the people around them, the happier they will be.

7. They grieve differently.

They move on quickly, they do whatever needs to be done in the moment of grief to get over it as quickly as possible, and then they try to look for the other happy things that are going on in their lives and focus on that instead.

8. They love with all their heart.

They are not afraid to take the risk of being *vulnerable* or giving their all to someone. They take chances and give even more chances. They know that opening themselves up is the only way to find true love.

9. They are not too hard on themselves.

They don't beat themselves up over their mistakes or poor choices. They don't look back and say *'I should've done that'* or *'I shouldn't have said that.'* They accept the fact that they are human beings susceptible to making mistakes and wrong decisions and they bounce back quickly from any misfortune they face.

10. They find something to look forward to.

They always find something to look forward to, no matter what it is. They find something to keep them motivated, excited, and *appreciative* of life.

11. They are genuinely happy for others.

They don't envy people or get jealous of their success, they celebrate with them too. They know that their day will come eventually and they want to see other people happy.

12. They don't compare.

They don't scroll down on social media and compare their lives to others. They strive for more while being happy with what they already have.

13. They embrace fear of the unknown.

They get comfortable with being a little uncomfortable. They keep a positive outlook in life and let the universe take care of the details.

14. They don't pay attention to what others think.

They don't focus on what people say about them or how they label them. They live their lives in a way that makes them truly happy and they take no notice of the *naysayers.*

15. They *choose* to be happy.

Ultimately, happiness is a choice not a mood. Nothing will go right all the time, but happy people choose to *stay* happy. They choose to wake up every day and decide to be happy no matter which side of the bed they woke up on.

44

14 Signs You Think With Your Heart Not Your Head

If you've been told you think with your heart, it means you make decisions and behave based on how you're feeling rather than what may be rational. It also means that your heart dictates your life in most occasions. Here are 14 other signs you are someone who thinks with their heart.

1. You wear your heart on your sleeve.

You tend to show your emotions easily and even when you are trying to hide what you are truly feeling, your *eyes* will give it all away eventually.

2. You blurt out more than you should.

You pour your heart out when you're having a conversation, it's how you bond with people. You prefer conversations that are deep, honest and meaningful even if it means revealing more than what people asked for.

3. You need a lot of time before making a decision.

It's easy to make a decision based on logic but making one based on fleeting emotions and feelings can take a totally different direction. You take your time to understand how you *feel* about something. But once you do, you know in your heart that it was the right choice – at least for you.

4. You get angry when you see dishonesty and injustice.

You are always trying to make the world a better place and it deeply saddens you when you see that other people are suffering because of someone else's wrongdoings.

5. You easily absorb the energy of those around you.

You don't know how to isolate yourself from the energy around you. You take it all in – more than you should because you are more *attuned* to emotions. Which can be a downfall if you don't look out for yourself and stop yielding to the energy of others.

6. You dream big.

If you think with your heart, that means you're both *passionate* and *empathetic,* this is why you have big dreams and want to touch the hearts of millions of people or change the world one day. You know that your heart will pave the way for you to do great things and you are constantly thinking of how you can put it to good use.

7. 'I feel like...' is your favorite sentence.

Forget *'I think that,'* it's all about how you feel and what triggers those feelings. Even when you are trying to solve a mathematical equation, you will always go with the answer that *feels* right.

8. You are a good friend.

Because you are highly intuitive and care about your friends, you are usually the person they go to when they really need to talk to someone or need support. They know that you will always make time for them and listen to them with all your *heart.*

9. You are spiritual.

You love nature and exploring the beauty of the world. You pay attention to the sounds of nature and you like to just daydream and contemplate for hours by yourself. You are totally fine with spending time alone to invigorate your heart.

10. You are highly creative or artistic.

You have a knack for art and appreciate the delicacies of it. You *feel* the passion that was behind a specific project and you relate to it so much more. You are either an artist or you have great potential to be one.

11. You are dynamic.

Because you can experience several emotions throughout the day, you are versatile and can find yourself getting involved in projects that are very different or hanging out with people who are polar opposites. But this what makes you an interesting individual, you are *unpredictable* – even to yourself.

12. You feel like an old soul.

Sometimes you look around and feel like you were born in the wrong era, you crave an era when life was simple and people were honest, or you crave the innocence of childhood when you *only* thought with your heart. Many times you *feel* like you don't belong to this generation.

13. You have a love-hate relationship with your brain.

You love it because it gives you the reality check you need and you hate it because it holds you back from being who you really are. You still haven't figured out a way to co-exist and you don't know if you ever will. Until then, your heart will always take over.

14. You will never give up on love.

No matter how many times your heart has been broken, no matter how many people disappointed you, no matter how many people told you to use your brain instead, you will always love *wholeheartedly* and think with your heart, even if it means hurting yourself, but you know that your heart is the force that keeps you going and it won't let you have it any other way.

45

20 Signs You're An Ambivert (Neither An Introvert Nor An Extrovert)

If you feel like you're not totally an introvert and not completely an extrovert, there is a new term for you...AMBIVERT.

Here are some signs you may actually be an ambivert.

1. You like attending big social gatherings and occasions but you don't necessarily start conversations or seek out new friendships.

2. But you are happy if people come and talk to you and you are more likely to engage in long conversations.

3. You don't like being alone for a long time, however you also get tired of going out regularly. Weekends are never predictable for you.

4. You know how to blend in really well with both introverts and extroverts and you have close friends of both types.

5. However, your friends probably won't get along without you.

6. You excel at both solo projects and team work and you are just as productive in both scenarios.

7. You still can't decide whether you're an introvert or an extrovert; neither can your friends.

8. You can't make solid decisions. Because part of you wants to slow things down and the other part wants to speed things up.

9. You are always the sound of wisdom for your friends. Because you have the perfect balance of both introverts and extroverts, they will both come to you for advice because you can relate to both.

10. You have fun partying and just as much fun grabbing coffee with a friend.

11. You can read people better than most as you can put yourself in their shoes for the most part.

12. You can be indecisive and find difficulty in expressing how you truly feel.

13. You probably know how to enjoy your time wherever you go because the usual things that drain an introvert or an extrovert don't drain you.

14. You are the prefect travel partner because you are more flexible and adaptable than most people.

15. You like being the center of attention sometimes, but too much of it makes you nervous.

16. You have a love-hate relationship with social media. Part of you wants to participate in it and the other is really indifferent about it.

17. You open up to people easily but it takes a while for you to trust someone.

18. You are a great partner because you will be able to provide the perfect balance of depth and playfulness.

19. Some days you blow up your friend's phones and other days you completely screen their calls.

20. You are not bipolar–you're just an ambivert!

46

29 Lessons About Life And Love I've Learned In 29 Years

1. You may not always get what you want in life, but sometimes this could be a blessing and a *sign* to steer yourself in another direction better than the one you were on.

2. You will struggle to define many things in your life, but in time you will realize that the real *meaning* of life is in the journey not in the definitions or the explanations.

3. Don't look for people to fix you, look for people who will stand beside you as you fix yourself.

4. Forgiving someone is not weakness; hating them is.

5. You can't take what other people say about you personally. What they think and say is a reflection of them, not you.

6. You are going to think that you know everything about love until you learn that love will never be *understood*.

7. Invest in a few good friends, they will always be your backbone and the ones you go to when you have no one else.

8. No matter how much progress you make, there will always be someone who thinks you are not good enough. Live to prove things to *yourself* not others.

9. Family matters, but they don't always know what matters to *you*. They can be wrong too. Don't blindly trust them.

10. At times you will wonder why bad things are happening to you, quit wondering and start enjoying the little things in life, when you get your answers, you will understand that these bad times were shaping you into the person you should be. **You have to fight through some bad days to earn the best days of your life.**

11. If nothing ever helps you, *music* surely will.

12. Your talent is God's gift to you, don't squander that gift, and hone your talent instead. There's a saying that says **"your gift will make a way for you."**

13. When you stop chasing the wrong things you give the right things a chance to catch you.

14. You will struggle to let go of someone, but you will realize that holding on is worse. Either way you have to learn how to let go of things that are not meant for you.

15. One book can change your life. Never underestimate the valuable lessons you can learn from one man's experiences.

16. You will learn that sometimes you have to be your only fan until you find your audience.

17. Don't be too hard on yourself if you think you pushed someone away. People who truly care about you will find a reason to stay.

18. It's OK to be guarded but don't deny love when you start feeling it. You will never regret taking a chance on love.

19. You will learn that you are stronger than you thought. You will learn that you are able to get through all your 'worst-case scenarios.'

20. Success only feels great when it's fused with *passion*.

21. Your looks won't define you but your character will. Always work on your character first.

22. If you get an opportunity to start over somewhere else–take it. It will change your life.

23. Difficult moments and scars will be merely stories to be told *proudly* to those who want to listen. Take pride in your scars.

24. Learn how to love your loneliness. If you are OK with being alone you will never fear the *void*.

25. Something will always scare you, even the things you wished for. Don't let fear cripple you from living the life you wanted. Let fear walk with you until it finds its own way.

26. You have to pray when things are good, not only when things are bad. Gratitude will give you more blessings. **Don't pray when it rains if you don't pray when the sun shines.**

27. Sometimes you have be vulnerable and say what you really feel. It will give you clarity, closure and peace of mind.

28. '*This too shall pass*' and '*life goes on*' are two timeless mantras you need to remember when times get rough.

29. Don't give up. Someone once said it's always the last key on the key ring that opens the door.

47

How To Write The Best Story Of Your Life

Each new day is an opportunity to write a new story; a blank page to start over and begin writing a new chapter. You have pages to fill with your own words. You have sentences to live by and characters to support your story. Make sure you write a story that you love, a story you are proud of, a story your children and grandchildren will want to read over and over again, and make sure you write an authentic one, an original one, a story that reflects your life, your dreams and your desires – not a copy of someone's life or a story someone else has written for you. Here is how to write the best story of your life.

Start by building the right characters.

Your characters are the ones that make your story come to life, and they are an integral part of your journey. Pick the right characters, the ones that will stick with you till the end of the story, the ones that will support you when your story is falling apart, the ones who will fill all your pages and chapters, and the ones who will help you write a happy ending.

Find the purpose of your story.

What are you trying to tell the world? What are you here for? And what story do you want people to read about you? Find a meaning to your story that makes you come alive and inspires you to wake up every day. Find a meaning that keeps your story interesting and keeps you *interested*, find a meaning to fight for, live for and die for.

Don't let defeat put an end to your story.

Every great story has periods of despair, failures and defeats, but this is what makes it even more compelling and this is what makes it even more substantial. This is the climax of your story and the turning point. This is when you start changing and your whole story changes. It now becomes about how you handle defeat, how you rise up after you fall down, and how you change the direction of your life after failure. A *victorious* ending requires a series of lost battles.

Pick an exciting theme.

The theme is one of the most fundamental components of your story. Pick a theme that ends each chapter with hope, faith, and a desire to make tomorrow better. A theme that makes your character stronger in every chapter, a theme that makes people root for you and want to see you make it to the end. Pick a positive theme, a humorous tone maybe, or a theme that depicts the strength in struggle and the beauty in vulnerability.

Love is the essence of your story.

Your story will be very weak without the power of love. You have to write a story of love and passion. Love is what keeps the story moving forward. It could be a lover, a friend, your work, your parents, your children, God or the love of the journey, the love of the unknown, or even your struggle to find love and define it. No matter how you tackle it, love is the *crux* of your story.

Don't worry so much about the ending.

Pay more attention to the *details* of your story and the way it's unfolding. The best writers often don't know how their story will end, they just start writing and the ending comes to them after they've shaped the main plot. If you focus too much on the ending, you might miss out on the whole story.

Give it a spectacular title.

The title is what summarizes your story in a few words. It's what makes people want to read your story. It's your choice how you want people to perceive your story. Each day you make a choice as to whether the title ends with a question mark, a period, or an exclamation point.

48

A Thank You Letter To All Those Who Told Me I Wasn't Good Enough

To the teacher who didn't think I was smart enough.

Thank you. It's because of you that I learned how to find my own idea of genius and find a path away from all the textbooks and tests that you thought were for everyone. It's because of you that I decided to find books that speak to my heart instead of studying books that never evoked my inspiration.

To the parent who didn't believe in me.

Thank you. It's because of you that I learned the art of rebellion. I learned that just because you brought me into this world doesn't mean you will lock me inside of it. I learned to find my own voice amidst all the *noise* you kept trying to tell me. I learned that if you do not lead by example, I am not obliged to follow you.

To the person who never loved me back.

Thank you. It's because of you I learned to love myself. I learned that I do not need your validation or your approval to believe that I am a person who deserve to be immensely loved. I learned that I will fall for a lot of boys who may not love me back, and I learned that as long as I don't lose myself in the process – love will always be an unpredictable yet delightful experience. I learned that I am capable of being on my own. I learned that I don't need a man to complete me.

To the friend who backstabbed me.

Thank you. It's because of you that I learned to be careful with who I trust. I learned to pick my friends wisely. I learned that people are not always as they may seem and I learned that some good friendships will end over the most trivial reasons.

To the boss who discounted my opinion.

Thank you. You forced me to find another job which made me find a better boss and a better path for me. Every time you would bring me down, I would find a way to build myself back up. You made me find my own identity, you made me walk away with pride. You pushed me to make my dreams happen so I don't have to ever work for someone like you again.

To the person who made fun of my dreams.

Thank you. You made me fight for them even more. By belittling me; you only belittled yourself. You made me realize that some people will always hate what they don't understand and some people are shallow enough to think that anything that seems unconventional will always be a failure. Thank you for teaching me how not to associate myself with people like you. Thank you for making fall in love with my dreams even more.

To the one who decided he can do better.

Thank you. You made me realize I *deserve* better. You made me put an end to all the excuses I made for people who didn't treat me well. You made me put an end to all the lies I told myself about people who were clearly wrong for me. And you made me stop trying to change myself for someone else. You made me believe in finding someone who falls in love with who I really am – with all my imperfections.

To anyone who will make me feel like I am not good enough.

Thank you in advance. Every time you doubt me, you make me believe in myself even more. Every time you belittle me, I love myself even more and every time you try to destroy me, you make me *invincible*.

<u>49</u>

10 Things God Wants You To Remember When Life Gets Rough

1. He is listening.

He is listening to your prayers, your fears, your pain and your silence. He is listening to what you are asking for and in time he will either give you what you were asking for or something much better.

2. He is making you stronger.

With every unanswered prayer, with every disappointment, with every hurdle, with every loss, he is making you stronger. He is giving you the strength you need so you can be strong for others. So you can be a strong mother, a strong father, a strong wife, a strong husband, a strong daughter, a strong son, and a strong friend.

3. He has a better plan for you.

He knows what's better for you, he knows what you *need* not what you *want*. He is planning the perfect timing for your life.

The timing of your love, the timing of your career, and the timing of your miracle.

4. He will answer your questions.

He will show you why you didn't get that job, or why it didn't work out with that person. He will show you why you lost a loved one, why he broke your heart or why he tested you so much. He will make things clear to you and you will thank him for it.

5. He will heal you.

He will heal your broken heart, he will ease your restless mind, and he will solve the mystery of your puzzled thoughts. He wants you to be patient but he will always *fix* you.

6. He wants you to trust him.

He wants you to have faith in him, he wants you to leave the big things – the uncontrollable things up to him, he wants you to believe in him, he wants you to go back to him when you think you have no one and he wants you to trust that he will provide for you when you lose everything. He will always rescue you before you drown.

7. He wants you to know you're never alone.

He is always there with you; when you're scared or confused, he is there with you. When you're afraid of the dark, he is there with you. When you are crying late at night and you think no one can hear you, he can hear you. When you've given up on your life and on love and think you have no one, you have him. No matter where you are, he is always with you and he wants you to trust that he is *enough*.

8. He wants you to grow.

He wants to you to change, he wants you to learn things the hard way, he wants you to evolve, he wants you step outside of your comfort zone, he wants you to lose your way so you can find him and find *yourself*. He wants you to be wise and strong and he wants you to prosper.

9. He wants you to know he loves you.

He loves you more than you know, he may be hard on you sometimes but he loves you, he may not give you everything you asked for but he loves you. No matter how many mistakes you've made or how many times you got angry with him, he still loves you, he forgives you and he is turning your life around. He doesn't love you for your money or your looks or your status, he loves you for you. *God loves you more in a moment than anyone could in a lifetime.*

10. He wants you to believe in miracles.

He is bringing you small miracles so you can believe in the

big miracles. In every dream of yours that come true, in every pleasant surprise you get, in every enlightening situation you encounter, in every person who moved you, in every person you loved – he's making miracles happen. He's a God of magic, wonder and hope and he wants you to believe that.

50

A Letter To My Future Old Self

I hope you're happy and healthy and I hope you finally managed to master all these hard yoga poses that you vowed to master one day.

I hope you wake up every morning smiling at the man you love; the one who made you realize that loving you was easy, the one who decided to be your best friend, the one who put an end to any addiction to self-loathe you may have had. I hope you are happily married to him and I hope you still laugh like you used to and still enjoy the simple moments with him. I hope you still look at each other the way you did when you fell in love and I hope you still hold his hand when you are crossing the street. I hope you still whisper sweet things to each other, and I hope his hug still warms your soul. But more importantly, I hope you realized that every time you worried about not finding love was a waste of time.

If you are not married, I hope you are happy by yourself, I hope you found amazing activities and projects to give love to, I hope you had an amazing career that you are proud of, and I hope you are strong and happy. I hope you realized that life is so much more than finding someone to love. I hope you finally fell in love with *yourself* and realized that this is essentially who you really needed to love.

I hope you look in the mirror and finally smile at your reflection, I hope you don't run away from mirrors anymore.

If you have kids, I hope you raised them to be strong and confident and taught them how to believe in themselves. I hope you raised them to follow their dreams and not settle for a boring life. But I hope you raised to be *kind* and compassionate, I hope you raised them in a way that they respect people and respect you. I hope you provided them with a home full of love, and gave them a beautiful meaning to the word *'family.'* I hope that every time they feel broken, your love makes them whole again. I hope you raised them in a way that you are proud of and a way that makes them happy.

If you don't have kids, I hope you are still in touch with your closest friends, and I hope you still find the same things you used to laugh at just as hilarious. I hope you call them often to check on them or call them just to remember the good old times. I hope you remember the hard times and laugh about how you used to stress over nothing, and I hope you realized that every second you spent investing in good friends was totally worth it. I hope you finally understood why things happened the way they did. I hope you got all the clarity you needed and all the closures you ever asked for. I hope you got your questions answered and I hope you are *satisfied* with the solutions.

I hope you ran into all those who hurt you once, and I hope you look at them without resentment. I hope you remember how they made you feel and not feel the bitterness that once consumed you. I hope you think of them as teachers who taught you lessons you wouldn't have learned otherwise. And I hope you understand that it was never about you – it was always *them*.

I hope you are still fun, I hope you still dance at weddings, sing at Karaoke bars and send silly selfies to your friends. I hope you never run of moments to make you feel alive or make you feel like a child again. I hope you still have a sense of humor about your flaws and I hope you finally learned how to love them. I hope you look in the mirror and finally smile at your reflection, I hope you don't run away from mirrors anymore.

I hope you still read life-changing books, and I hope you still find new lessons to learn and new things to learn about yourself. I hope you never stopped learning or growing or evolving. I hope you finally wrote that book or that memoir or produced that TV show. I hope you documented your life somehow, I hope you shared your life with strangers, and I hope you still tell them stories about your life and listen to theirs. I hope you never lose your love for deep conversations, and I hope you always find the right words to say.
I hope you reached your final destination and now you travel to travel instead of traveling to run away from something or try to find yourself.

I hope you finally traveled to all those places you wanted to visit, and I hope you found beauty and wonder in all your travels. I hope you came back a better person, a happier person, and a more grateful person. But I hope you learned that the real journey is the one within, and I hope you reached your final destination and now you travel to travel instead of traveling to run away from something or try to find yourself.

I hope that when you are sitting by the window looking at the amazing view from your balcony, you look back on your life and smile. I hope you look back and realize that you made the best out of what you were given, that you learned the lessons you needed to learn, that you finally let go of what was not meant to be and embraced the *uncertainty* of life. I hope you look back and remember the days you laughed and the happy memories, I hope you remember the people who loved you and were there for you, and I hope you finally forgave the ones who didn't and *detoxified* your heart.

I hope you are not scared of *death,* I hope you lived in a way that made you unafraid of death, and I hope you have no regrets. I hope you leave something wonderful for the world to remember you by and I hope you leave the world remembering that it was *wonderful.*

Thought Catalog, it's a website.

www.thoughtcatalog.com

Social

facebook.com/thoughtcatalog
twitter.com/thoughtcatalog
tumblr.com/thoughtcatalog
instagram.com/thoughtcatalog

Corporate

www.thought.is

Made in the USA
Lexington, KY
07 June 2017